THE
COACH TO COUCH
QUIZ BOOK

Simon Hollingsworth

Dedicated to Sheila

INTRODUCTION

It's all Jen's fault, this book.

The lockdown began and my chum Jen thought it would be a good idea to get pals together on Zoom calls to beat the boredom and the loneliness with some quizzing. Friends from around the world thought this would be a good idea, and the first quiz was a great success.

Jen asked if anyone else wanted a go at hosting, and with another hiatus on the real-work front, I readily agreed. My offspring Ksenia was locked down with me, and we could devise something together for a laugh.

After my first venture, I followed Jen's lead by offering the reins to anyone else wanting an alternative to *Homes Under the Hammer* reruns, to be met by the online sound of tumbleweed. So, I did another quiz and then another 64. I did it in two languages for a while, drew my own quiz pictures, learned all manner of useless stuff and never offered the reins to anyone again.

This little institution provided up to 100 people something to do on 65 consecutive Sundays until I realised that Covid restrictions had been lifted and I had a life. Finding myself with an archive of material and a wonderful boozer with no regular quiz, not a minute's walk away, I decided to try my daft questions on a new audience.

And the Monday night quiz at the Old Coach House in Southwell was born.

Having passed the 100th quiz down the pub, where I get paid in beer and where my ego is fed by ripples of applause and the use of a microphone, I thought it would be a nice idea to spread the joy a little further. Or perhaps I am getting ideas above my station, and the only people who'll take an interest will be the pub's regulars, the online quizzers once I plug this book to them and my Mum and Dad, who, I fear, already know what they're getting for Christmas.

Oh, and Jen, too.

This is a quiz book, so I'll get to the questions in a moment, but I have to thank several people, without whom many would have found something else to do over the lockdown or another quieter pub to frequent on a Monday night.

A special thank you to Cherrie Rollerson and Colin Rodger, landlords past and present of The Old Coach House in Southwell, for putting up with me talking sphericals for a couple of hours every week. A big thank you to the regular teams, both online and in the pub, without whom I wouldn't have half the inspiration for the new material I keep churning out. You know who you are, you eclectic silly fecn bandits, you musketeers behaving politely, you strontium bar flies from 1986, you clueless coughers, Stevie Nix and, of course, Arlo the dog.

Oh, and Jen, too.

THE QUIZZES

This is a compilation of my first fifty quizzes down the pub from the beginning, incorporating much of the material from the initial online version and plenty of new stuff.

The quizzes follow a regular pattern with six rounds on different subjects. The first five rounds feature five questions on a given theme, while the sixth round is a connections round, where I pose six general knowledge questions that are unrelated, but their answers have a connection. You have to work out the connection.

Where rounds are specific to a particular date, such as quirky news of the week, I have given the date for a bit of context.

In researching these questions, I have always done my best to make them original, and the inspiration has come from friends, family, fellow quizzers, overheard conversations and even the sit-up-in-bed-at-3 a.m. flashes of whatever flashes at 3 a.m. Most of this drivel is unique drivel, and I hope you find it informative, useful, entertaining, or, at the very least, heatproof for that mug of tea you're looking to put down.

I always ask for suggested rounds for birthdays, anniversaries, favourite subjects and so on. Once, I asked a team on a winning streak what they were bad at, and they replied, 'girlfriends'. And so, the round on failed relationships was born, which appears in this book.

I hope you'll find something to suit everyone, from regular sport, history, science and literature to word and picture conundrums, memes, sidekicks, biscuits, beer and dumplings.

I hope you enjoy and, if you don't, remember: it's all Jen's fault.

QUIZ No. 1

Round 1
The Cherrie Round

As a special thank you to Cherrie for letting me host my quiz in the best pub in town, this round is dedicated to you! All the answers feature cherries or people with a name that sounds identical, even though it might be spelt differently.

Q1. Who wrote the play called *The Cherry Orchard*?

Q2. What was the name of the manufacturer of the Cherry 100A in the 1970s?

Q3. What is the surname of the family that lives at 17 Cherry Tree Lane?

Q4. This cherry is tart and red-gold, and it is popular in baking. The name is shared with a monarch who came to the throne in 1702. What is it called?

Q5. Name the bright red cherry type that shares its name with one half of the brand name of a cigarette, which has AND in the middle.

Round 2
Robin Hood

Q6. In the famous legend, whom does Robin meet at the River Leen?

Q7. According to the legend, in what village was Robin Hood born?

Q8. What is the name of the wandering minstrel who became a member of the band of outlaws?

Q9. The famous oak tree in Sherwood Forest is known by what adjective?

Q10. Which one of Robin Hood's Merry Men has been played in film by Ray Winstone, Christian Slater and Jamie Dornan?

Round 3

Bridges

Q11. Name this bridge. It separates a country from an island.

Q12. This bridge features in which famous film?

Q13. Here is an image from a famous film that contains the word BRIDGE in the title. What is that film?

Q14. Here is my reproduction of a famous war film that contains THAT word. Name the film.

"A MAGNIFICENT, MOVING FILM!"
"DESTINED TO BECOME A CLASSIC!"

Q15. Here's another type of Bridge. This one is Jeff Bridges, starring in one of his best-loved films. What is it called?

Round 4
Sport
Q16. What nationality is tennis player Novak Djokovic?
Q17. Two of the three weapons used in modern fencing are EPEE and FOIL. What is the third?
Q18. Which watch brand is the sponsor of the referee boards in FIFA tournaments?
Q19. A famous sportsperson has a tattoo on his right arm that reads POWER and another on his left arm that reads GLORY. What is his name?
Q20. Winners of the World Championship, the UK Championship and the Masters now sport a three-pronged crown on their clothing when competing. About which sport am I talking?

Round 5
Rhyming destinations
Each of these maps highlights journeys between places that rhyme with each other. Examples could be Bali to Mali, Crewe to Looe and so on. They could be names of countries or names or cities.

Q21.

Q22.

Q24.

Q23.

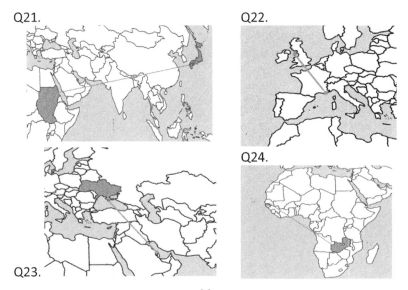

Q25.

Round 6
Connections

Q26. Which popular Disney character has been played in film by Kristen Stewart, Lily Collins and Elizabeth McGovern?

Q27. Who wrote the songs *Swallowed in the Sea*, *Magic* and *Fix You* for his wife?

Q28. What unit would give a 1-kg mass an acceleration of one metre per second per second?

Q29. Who wrote a famous opera about a legendary, crossbow-wielding folk hero of Switzerland?

Q30. The Scottish economist Smith, the American actor Driver and the Polish poet Mickiewicz all share what?

Q31. What popular baked sweet or savoury dish takes its name from the German word for 'whirlpool'?

Q32. What is the connection?

QUIZ No. 2

Round 1
Halloween

Q1. Jadis is the White Witch in what famous series of children's books?

Q2. Helen Nicoll gave us a series of children's books about a well-meaning witch, her striped cat, and their friend Owl. What were the books called?

Q3. *Bates Motel* starring Freddie Highmore is the prequel to what classic horror film?

Q4. 'An invisible man, sleeping in your bed' is a lyric from what hit belonging to the '80s movie of the same title?

Q5. Billy Corgan is the lead singer of which Halloween-sounding group?

Round 2
Sequences

Complete the following sequences.

Q6. PAUL, GEORGE, JOHN, _____

Q7. After I, V and X, what is the next Roman numeral of one character?

Q8. Maths sequence: 1, 8, 27, ___

Q9. Sport sequence: 1, 18, 4, 13, ___

Q10. A film sequence for you now. Give me the two letters that come next in this sequence.

SC, GL, RM, TD, PB, ___

Round 3
Plants in books and films

Q11. I think you know what these are. However, the question is this. What film containing this plant won the Best Picture Oscar?

Q12. Who starred in the leading role in the 1951 film whose title contains this plant?

Q13. What Harry Potter character shares a name with this plant?

Q14. The central character of this famous book is called Tom Joad. The book's title contains this plant. What is the name of the book?

Q15. Name the famous film that stars Shirley MacLaine, Sally Field and Dolly Parton and features this plant.

Round 4
Politics

Q16. In 1981, the so-called Gang of Four broke away from the Labour Party to form the Social Democratic Party or SDP. Three of the four were men (Roy Jenkins, David Owen and Bill Rodgers), but who was the woman member of the Gang of Four?

Q17. Who is the current leader of the Liberal Democrats?

Q18. Of all the British prime ministers, only two have a surname that contains three letters. One is Andrew Bonar Law (and even then, I think 'Bonar' is part of his surname). Who is the other?

Q19. Who was Britain's last Liberal Prime Minister?

Q20. Complete the following sentence: 'Spencer Perceval is the only serving British Prime Minister to _____.'

Round 5
Mashups of famous relations
To get the point, name both people you can see.

Q21.

Q22.

Q23.

Q24.

Q25.

Round 6
Connections
Q26. In what film does Vin Diesel voice the character Groot and Bradley Cooper voice the character Rocket Raccoon?

Q27. The name of this river translates as 'River of Silver'. The port of Montevideo stands on its estuary. What is the name of this river in English?

Q28. Which word that begins with 'R' follows TAIL, TURBINE and HELICOPTER?

Q29. Gerard Butler stars in the film 300 as the king of what ancient city-state?

Q30. To whom did the apostle Paul send epistles, raising concerns surrounding a Christian community in Greece?
Q31. This Portuguese explorer, the 1st Count of Vidigueira, was the first European to reach India by sea. What was his name?
Q32. What is the connection?

QUIZ No. 3

Round 1
Songs and colours
Name the song. Each title contains a colour.

Q1.   How does it feel
       When you treat me like you do
       And you've laid your hands upon me
       And told me who you are?

       Q2.   Every time just like the last
              On her ship tied to the mast
              To distant lands
              Takes both my hands
              Never a frown with BLANK BLANK

Q3.   Always believe in your soul
       You've got the power to know
       You're indestructible
       Always believe in
       'Cause you are BLANK

       Q4.   Past the square, past the bridge
              Past the mills, past the stacks
              On a gathering storm
              Comes a tall handsome man
              In a dusty black coat with
              A BLANK BLANK hand

Q5.   But I will go down with this ship
       And I won't put my hands up and surrender
       There will be no BLANK BLANK above my door
       I'm in love and always will be

Round 2
All about fire
Q6. What is a weather phenomenon, often seen at sea, a song by John Parr and a film by Joel Schumacher?

Q7. Which leader allegedly played the violin while his capital city burned?

Q8. What is the name of the film about two athletes at the 1924 Olympics? The title contains the word FIRE.

Q9. On what street did the Great Fire of London start?

Q10. This chap's first name was actually Paul. He was a pioneering American oil well firefighter who became notable for extinguishing and capping oil well fires. The John Wayne film Hellfighters was loosely based on his life. By what name do we know him best?

Round 3
Famous people superimposed onto famous portraits

Can you name the subject of the portrait and the superimposed person?

Q11.   Q12.   Q13.

Q14.   Q15.

Round 4
Racket sports
Q16. Which racket sport shares its name with famous horse trials held in Gloucestershire every April or May?
Q17. When Boris Johnson suggested that the sport of Table Tennis would be coming home, what name did he give it? In other words, he didn't call it 'Table Tennis'.
Q18. Egypt accounts for 7 of the top 10 men's players and 6 of the top 10 women's players in which racket sport?
Q19. Sam Groth holds what world record in tennis?
Q20. The tennis player Marin Cilic comes from what country?

Round 5
Monuments and memorials

Q21. What is this monument called?

Q22. This one looks similar to the one before. One of its names is Constitution Arch. The other name is taken from the name of the man whose famous battle victory is commemorated with this arch. What is that other name?

Q23. Name the city where you can see this extensive Holocaust memorial.

Q24. Who is buried in the rectangle in the foreground of this picture?

Q25. A famous Holocaust memorial comprises bronze casts of shoes left behind by victims. On the banks of which river can you find this unique memorial?

Round 6
Connections

Q26. Who holds the world record for the 100 and 200 metres sprints?

Q27. What group performed the theme song to the James Bond film *Live and Let Die*?

Q28. If Red is for Office, Green is for Xboxnd Yellow is for Bing, what is Blue for?

Q29. Sir Lindsay Hoyle holds what post in the Houses of Parliament?

Q30. What is the collective name for the islands that form a line running south from Miami in the United States?

Q31. What do the logos of Delta Airlines, Google Play and Mitsubishi all have in common?

Q32. What is the connection?

QUIZ No. 4

Round 1
Cocktails

Q1. Which cocktail mixes vodka and orange juice in a highball glass?
Q2. This cocktail contains brandy, Cointreau and lemon juice. What is it called?
Q3. Which cocktail contains equal proportions of gin, Campari and vermouth and is served with a garnish of orange peel?
Q4. Who invented the Vesper cocktail, which contains gin, vodka and Kina Lillet or Cocchi Americano?
Q5. The popular cocktail Sex on the Beach contains vodka, peach schnapps, orange juice and what other juice?

Round 2
The One-letter round

Q6. Josh Brolin starred in a presidential biopic containing a single letter representing that president's middle initial. Which letter?
Q7. Will Smith's character in *Men in Black* is known by what one letter?
Q8. What computer language was first developed in 1972?
Q9. In Berlin, the U-Bahn is the equivalent of our underground in London. What letter is given to signify the overground trains in Berlin and other major German cities?
Q10. Desmond Llewelyn played what famous role in 17 films?

Round 3
World's largest

Q11. What is the name of this library, considered by many to be the largest library in the world?

Q12. This is a sketch of the world's largest sports stadium, with a capacity of about 116,000 people. In which country would you find it?

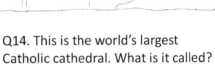

Q13. This is the world's tallest clock tower. In which country would you find it?

Q14. This is the world's largest Catholic cathedral. What is it called?

Q15. This is one of the world's largest what?

Round 4
The Poland round
Q16. Lech Walesa headed the Solidarity movement in the late 1980s in Poland, which started life in which major Polish shipyard town?
Q17. The town of Gniezno was Poland's first what?
Q18. Name the famous Polish composer whose Minute Waltz is used for the popular radio programme Just a Minute.
Q19. Many people think this was first consumed in Russia, but the Poles consumed it, allegedly for medicinal purposes, in the 11th century. Its name means water in the native language. What product am I talking about?
Q20. In Poland, you can visit Malbork, the world's largest building of its kind and the world's largest brick-built building. But what type of building is it?

Round 5
Name the car from the grille
Q21.

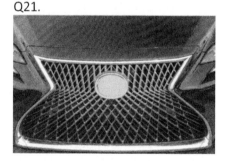

Q22.

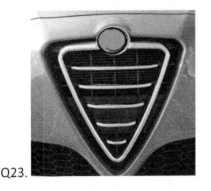
Q23.

Q24.

Q25.

Round 6
Connections

Q26. Recurve, Long, Mongolian and Cross are all types of what?

Q27. In London, by what name are the A205 and A406 better known?

Q28. What is the length between two wickets in cricket called?

Q29. A standard guitar has 20 vertical lines on it. Some guitars have up to 24 vertical lines. What are these lines called?

Q30. A popular dance in Scotland in the 16th and 17th centuries and in Ireland since the 18th century. It is an improvised dance performed with rapid footwork and a rigid torso. What is it called?

Q31. The Pope might wear a Camaouro, a Saturno or a Zucchetto on his head for different occasions. What would he wear for the most important ceremonies?

Q32. What is the connection?

QUIZ No. 5

Round 1
Sport and games in film
Q1. *Field of Dreams* is a famous film about what sport?
Q2. The 2017 film *I, Tonya*, starring Margo Robbie, is about what sport?
Q3. *Rush* is a 2013 film about Formula One motor racing. Name the two drivers about whose famous feud the film was made—½ point for each correct answer.
Q4. *The Color of Money*, starring Tom Cruise, is all about Pool. It is the sequel to a famous film about pool starring Paul Newman. What is that film called?
Q5. What board game was the subject of the popular Netflix series *The Queen's Gambit*?

Round 2
Wordplay in confectionery
Give me the names of well-known confectionery products from these clues. For example, if I said, 'Speak in a hushed tone', the answer would be 'Wispa'. Easy, right?
Q6. Talking point
Q7. A breed of dog
Q8. Above-average right of way
Q9. Smothered laughs
Q10. A price on someone's head

Round 3
Coats of arms

Q11. Here's a family coat of arms. What is the family name?

Q12. What is the family name represented by the coat of arms below?

Q13. Here is a coat of arms of a political party with the party symbol removed. Name the political party.

Q14. This is a country's coat of arms. Name the country

Q15. Whose coat of arms is this?

Round 4
Funny SUN newspaper headlines

As you know, many national newspapers enjoy playing with words in their headlines or employing funny-sounding titles. This little round is about this, where headlines are based on historical events.

Q16. Complete the famous Sun newspaper headline: FREDDIE STARR ATE MY _____

Q17. An April 2021 edition of the SUN had the headline BROTHERS AT ARMS LENGTH. About which brothers was this headline written?

Q18. About which sportsman did the Sun produce the headlines IT HAD TO BE CHEW! and GNASH OF THE DAY?

Q19. Someone clever has devised pretend Sun headlines for events further back In history. Here is one. CARDIGAN UNDONE AT BALACLAVA is a pretend headline about which famous war?

Q20. Arguably, the most famous sporting headline ever refers to Inverness Caledonian Thistle's shock 3-1 Scottish Cup win over Celtic in 2000. What was that headline?

Round 5
Famous residences

Q21. This is the second most visited house in the United States after the White House. What is it called?

Q22. This is the official seat of the mayor of which English city? Interestingly, Adolf Hitler planned to use this building as his headquarters for the UK branch of the Third Reich in the event of him winning the war.

Q23. This is the official residence of a world leader. What is the name of the building?

Q24. Here is another royal residence. What is it called?

Q25. In Key West, Florida, this house was used in Timothy Dalton's last outing as James Bond in the film *Licence to Kill*. The house was the private residence of what famous writer?

Round 6
Connections

Q26. What word, derived from two German words, means a biologically identical image of oneself, often equated in literature with a harbinger of bad luck or an evil twin?

Q27. 'When I called you last night from Glasgow' is a line from what famous song?

Q28. Which actor connects *The Mask of Zorro* and the Shrek spin-off *Puss In Boots*?

Q29. Anagram time. VISCOSE MEAT is an anagram of what medical procedures?

Q30. What was the name of the four-wheeled vehicle of Bruce Wayne's alter-ego?

Q31. What DIY store is the UK's number 1 trade catalogue outlet?

Q32. So, what's the connection?

QUIZ No. 6
(Mid-December) 2021

Round 1
Christmas cracker jokes
With Christmas just around the corner, I am sure you are all looking forward to pulling crackers and laughing your stockings off at the wild hilarity of the jokes inside.

To get you in the mood, I thought we'd have a round of cracker jokes, only you have to give me the punchline for the point. These are actual cracker jokes, so don't blame me when you start groaning.

Q1. What do you get when you cross a snowman with a vampire?

Q2. What do you get if you eat Christmas decorations?

Q3. How does Good King Wenceslas like his pizzas?

Q4. Why couldn't the skeleton go to the Christmas Party?

Q5. How did Mary and Joseph know that Jesus was 7lb 6oz when he was born?

Round 2
Extremes
Q6. If I were to ask you to name the tallest mountain in the world, you would probably tell me it's Everest. Everest is indeed the highest point above sea level, at 29,029 feet, but it is not the tallest mountain. That honour goes to Mauna Kea, at 35,500 feet, much of which is below sea level. On which island is Mauna Kea located?

Q7. According to NASA, the Atacama Desert is the driest place on Earth. In which country is this desert located?

Q8. What is the name of the world's tallest active volcano?

Q9. What body of water is the oldest and deepest lake in the world, estimated to contain one-fifth of the world's freshwater?

Q10. According to the World Economic Forum, what capital city is the densest in the world, with more than 44,000 people per square kilometre?

Round 3
Santa pictures.
I have messed around with Paint on my computer, disguising famous people in Santa outfits. You have to tell me who they are.

Q11.

Q12.

Q13.   Q14.

Q15.

Round 4
National dishes
Let's see how well you know your world food.

Q16. Moussaka is a bit like lasagne, only it uses aubergines. What country has moussaka as its national dish?

Q17. A popular rice dish, similar to Spanish Paella, only usually a little spicier, is the favourite dish in Louisiana. What is it called?

Q18. Khachapuri is a bread dish served with salty cheese on top or inside. Some variations involve a fried egg on top. In what country is Khachapuri a national dish?

Q19. Surstromming is a fermented herring dish with arguably the most disgusting smell of all food. What country has it as a national dish?

Q20. Hungary's national dish is a tomato-paprika meat stew. What is it called?

Round 5
Dingbats

Q21. Here is a well-known phrase or saying. What is it?

Q22. This is a British TV comedy programme. Name it.

	Team	P	W	D	L	GD	Pts
1	Charles	22	18	1	3	32	55
2	Alan	22	14	5	3	27	47
3	Timothy	22	13	7	2	29	46
4	Lee	22	13	6	3	24	45
5	Michael	22	13	4	5	15	43

Q23. Here is a famous film in code. Name that film.

COLIN M
COLIN MON
COLIN MONTG
COLIN MONTGOM
COLIN MONTGOMERIE ←

Q24. Another film title now. Name the film.

Salsa
Timber
Rumba
Grey
Tango

Q25. A song title for you to name now

TOSYOBEHTWN

Round 6
Connections

Q26. What word connects a product advertised by Gary Lineker and a breakfast presenter called Dan?

Q27. What is the first name of Boris Johnson's father?

Q28. What is not required in a famous Phil Collins album?

Q29. Which British king was a grandson of Queen Victoria and died in 1936?

Q30. What word connects a medal for prominent mathematicians and the actresses Sally and Gracie?

Q31. What colour is a song by Coldplay, a river in China and the colour of mourning in Mexico and Egypt?

Q32. So, what's the connection?

QUIZ No. 7
(20 December 2021)

Round 1
Christmas Number Ones
Q1. What boyband had the Christmas number one in 1994 with the song *Stay Another Day*?
Q2. Who had the Christmas number one in 1982 with the cheesy song *Save Your Love*?
Q3. The song *Only You* was written by Vince Clarke for Yazoo. However, it was a Christmas number one in 1983 for another performer who sang it a capella. What was the name of that group?
Q4. Bennie Hill had the Christmas number one in 1971 with what ridiculous song?
Q5. Girls Aloud had the Christmas number one in 2002, but with which song?

Round 2
Film title puns
This round is all about taking a film title and changing just one letter in the title to make a pun. So, I give you a clue, and you give me the film title and the pun title. To make it a bit easier, here's a clue. HORRIBLE FIZZY ORANGE DRINK would be BAD SANTA/BAD FANTA. Oh, and all these are Christmas films. Of course, they are.
Q6. TEETH-BREAKING PASTRY DISH EATEN ON A SKYSCRAPER
Q7. MORE LIKE WEST BRIGHTON, REALLY
Q8. THIS IS A SPECTACULAR GREEN CITRUS FRUIT
Q9. ARRIVE WITHOUT FRIENDS OR FAMILY
Q10. A YULETIDE SONG ABOUT THE STAR OF THE AMERICAN OFFICE?

Round 3
Is it this, or is it that?

Q11. Is this a loaf of bread or a corgi's bottom?

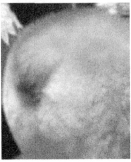

Q12. Are these pieces of fried chicken or labradoodles?

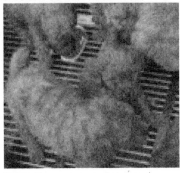

Q13. Are these pieces of fried chicken or labradoodles?

Q14. How many pictures here contain dalmatians?

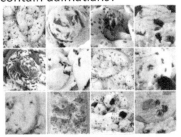

Q15. How many pictures here contain chihuahuas, as opposed to chocolate-chip cookies?

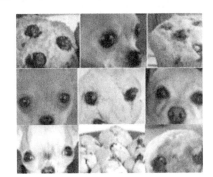

Round 4
A mixed bag of silliness
Q16. What is an INTERROBANG?
Q17. A COCKCHAFER is a species of what?
Q18. Frozen cow dung was the first material used for what sporting equipment?
Q19. A BLESSING, a MARVEL and a GLORY are all the collective terms for what?
Q20. What well-known fictional TV character is required to have sex once every seven years?

Round 5
Odd-one out round
Who or what is the odd one in each picture, and why?

Q21.

Q22.

Q23.

Q24.

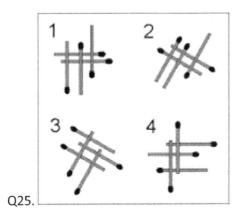

Q25.

Round 6
Connections

Q26. What is the metal or wooden mould that cobblers use to make shoes?

Q27. What is the popular late 1970s and 1980s American detective series about a wealthy couple and their jet-set lifestyle who often get embroiled in amateur sleuthing? They have a driver, troubleshooter and majordomo, Max, who narrates the stories.

Q28. Formerly known as Littlewoods Direct, what is the name of the online retailer with a pink square logo with a single word in white?

Q29. Also on the theme of retailers, the men's outfitters Hepworths was rebranded in the early 1980s to become which now-established High Street name?

Q30. What is the surname of the snooker player Ryan and the former Question Time presenter Robin?

Q31. What is produced by the lacrymal gland?

Q32. So, what's the connection?

QUIZ No. 8
(29 December 2021)

Round 1
Christmas song lyrics
Name the songs with the following lyrics.

Q1.
Where the treetops glisten and children listen
To hear sleigh bells in the snow.

Q2.
There must have been some magic in that old silk hat they found,
For when they placed it on his head, he began to dance around!

Q3.
Light and life to all he brings,
Risen with healing in his wings
Mild he lays his glory by,
Born that man no more may die.

Q4.
A pair of hopalong boots and a pistol that shoots
Is the wish of Barney and Ben;
Dolls that will talk and will go for a walk
Is the hope of Janice and Jen;
And Mom and Dad can hardly wait for school to start again.

Q5.
They looked up and saw a star
Shining in the east beyond them far,
And to the earth it gave great light,
And so it continued both day and night.

Round 2
Christmas plants
Q6. What is the name of the parasitic plant with green leaves and pearlescent berries that is a popular decoration for Christmas?
Q7. What is the name of the plant that the Druids regarded as a symbol of fertility and eternal life, thought to have magical powers,

while Christians see it as symbolising Christ's crown of thorns and his blood?

Q8. Which country sends a Christmas tree to the Queen every year as thanks for the UK's support during the Second World War?

Q9. IAN TIPTOES is an anagram of what popular Christmas-time plant?

Q10. These flower buds from an evergreen tree are used in whole or ground form in numerous Christmas recipes, including hot beverages. What are they called?

Round 3
Christmas film posters

Name the films from these posters with words or parts missing.

Q11.   Q12.   Q13.

Q14.   Q15.

Round 4
Christmas trivia

Q16. In the song *The Twelve Days of Christmas*, what was the gift given on the seventh day?

Q17. In *Home Alone 2*, into whom does Kevin run in the hotel lobby?

Q18. In which Christmas movie does Tom Hanks play 6 of the characters?
Q19. In what country did eggnog originate?
Q20. What country started the tradition of putting up a Christmas tree?

Round 5
Christmas dingbats
Q21. What Christmas word is found in this clue?

ABCDEFGHIJKMNOPQRSTUVWXYZ

Q22. What Christmas activity is this?

Pres   ents

Q23. What Christmas food is this?

Spear	Cottage
Pepper	Shepherd
Garden	Apple

Q24. Name the book and film from this picture clue

Q25. What Christmas item is this?

A3 Tortilla A4

Round 6
Connections
Q26. What TV sitcom focused on the Boswell family in Liverpool?
Q27. In which capital city would you find the statue of the Mannekin Pis, the boy piddling into a fountain?
Q28. The football teams Galatasaray and Besiktas play in which country?
Q29. In the children's book Charlotte's Web, who or what is Wilbur?
Q30. Who performs the popular song *Zombie*?
Q31. Of the six principal suspects in Cluedo, which one wears purple?
Q32. So, what's the connection?

QUIZ No. 9
(New Year's Special)

Round 1
Famous events on Jan 1st
Q1. Which duet had the number one single as of 1st January 2022?
Q2. On 1st January 1962, Decca Records famously said that who had no future in show business?
Q3. On 1st January 1660, which civil servant made the first entry in his diary?
Q4. BBC's *Top of the Pops* launched on January 1st in which year?
Q5. In 1892, this island opened a US immigration centre. What is the name of this island?

Round 2
Board games
Q6. When two players place red and yellow disks into a blue frame, what are they playing?
Q7. What is the name of the board game that features Liberals and Fascists, where the Liberals enact five policies or kill the Fascist Leader, or where the Fascist leader is elected Chancellor?
Q8. What board game features triangles, quadrants and even a bar?
Q9. What board game translates from Latin as I PLAY?
Q10. What game utilises sixteen dice in a 4×4 grid?

Round 3
Film posters in my drawings
Just name the films from these sketches of partial film posters.

Q11.　　　　　Q12.　　　　Q13.

 Q14.  Q15.

Round 4
One-line film synopses

Q16. Name this war film from the following one-line synopsis I have penned:

DRUGGED-UP ADOLESCENT CHUCKS FRISBEE TO DEFEAT NAZIS

Q17. Here's another. Name the film.

GREATEST SHOWMAN HIDES FROM GLADIATOR BECAUSE BATMAN'S GIRLFRIEND LEFT A CHILD AT ALI G's HOUSE

Q18. And another:

REDGRAVE ATTACKS BARRIERS WITH OIL DRUMS

Q19. Animated film title now

ADORABLE TRASH CAN AND FLOWERPOT FORCE FAT PEOPLE TO WALK

Q20. A Disney classic for you now

AFTER LOSING HIS FATHER, SON JOINS A HIPPY GROUP AND BECOMES A VEGAN

Round 5
Badges of sporting teams
Just name the teams with these badges

 Q21.  Q22.   Q23.

Q24. Q25.

Round 6
Connections
Q26. What accounts for 99.86% of the mass in the solar system?

Q27. In the 2010 animated film, what does Viking teenager Hiccup decide to train?

Q28. What is the highest award the British government bestows for non-operational gallantry or gallantry not in the presence of an enemy?

Q29. At 563.35 carats, the world's largest sapphire is the WHAT of India?

Q30. This man is Russian, and his first name is Mikhail. About 72 million of the weapon he invented have been built and are used worldwide. What is his surname?

Q31. The trees known as Acer and Sycamore are in which family of trees?

Q32. So, what's the connection?

QUIZ No. 10

Round 1
Disney
Q1. Which of Snow White's Seven Dwarves has the longest name?
Q2. Name the only Disney princess to sport a tattoo
Q3. Which Disney film is set in Paris and focuses on fine cuisine?
Q4. What famous story, adapted into a Disney classic, features the Darling family?
Q5. 50/50 chance at this one: which of Captain Hook's hands has been replaced by a hook?

Round 2
All about dumplings
Q6. Gyozas are steamed, fried or boiled dumplings with various fillings, but from which country do they hail?
Q7. Kreplach are usually triangular-shaped dumplings. What country calls them home?
Q8. Blodpalt is dark, filled dumplings made of rye bread and animal blood. Name one of their two countries of origin.
Q9. The belly button of Botticelli's Venus is said to have inspired what popular filled pasta dumpling?
Q10. What is the name of the triangular fried dumpling from the Indian subcontinent, usually stuffed with mince, potatoes, other vegetables and spices?

Round 3
Wrong heads
Name the two people pictured in each of these images

Q11.   Q12.   Q13.

Q14.   Q15.

Round 4
Famous people known only by their initials

Q16. The writer of *The Invisible Man* has the first name Herbert, but we know him best by his first two initials and surname. Name the two initials and surname.

Q17. There's another Herbert in the initials of the man who wrote *Sons and Lovers* and *Women in Love*. Who is he?

Q18. Name the singer and gay icon whose most famous song is the Grammy-winning *Constant Craving*. She is known by two initials and a surname.

Q19. 'When Father is taken away unexpectedly, Roberta, Peter, Phyllis and their mother have to leave their comfortable life in London to go and live in a small cottage in the country.' This is a one-line summary of a famous book by a woman whom we know by her initial and surname. What is that initial and surname?

Q20. The first name of the founder of Scientology is Lafayette, but he only uses the L in his name. What is the rest of his name?

Round 5
Cats
Name these breeds
Q21.

Q22.

Q23.

Q24.

Q25.

Round 6
Connections
Q26. Who wrote the novels about the character Jack Ryan? He has been played in film by Harrison Ford, Ben Affleck and John Krasinski, among others.
Q27. Where can you find Left Field, Pyramid, Silver Hayes and Shangri-La once every year?
Q28. Which Yorkshire seaside town is divided in two by the River Esk?
Q29. Name the long blond-haired crooner who has performed the songs *How am I supposed to live without you? Said I loved you... but I lied* and *How can we be lovers?*
Q30. What well-known palace features the Victoria Tower, the Elizabeth Tower and the Central Tower?
Q31. What race has a maximum of 40 runners and saw the same winner in 2018 and 2019?
Q32. So, what's the connection?

QUIZ No. 11

Round 1
Science
Q1. Nowadays, everyone seems to be a qualified immunologist, so this first question should be a doddle. A British scientist pioneered the concept of vaccines, including the world's first vaccine to combat smallpox. What was his name?

Q2. $a^2 + b^2 = c^2$ is better known as what mathematical theory?

Q3. What prominent scientist stated:
> 'I have noticed that even people who claim everything is predetermined and that we can do nothing to change it look before they cross the road'?

Q4. In 2012, scientists confirmed the detection of the long-sought Higgs boson at the Large Hadron Collider, the most powerful particle accelerator on the planet. This particle helps give mass to all elementary particles, such as electrons and protons. This particle has a nickname: it is called the _____ Particle. What is the missing word?

Q5. Sir Isaac Newton was an English mathematician, physicist, astronomer, theologian, and author. He was born and raised in a manor house, not a million miles from the Old Coach House in Southwell. What is the nearest town to that manor house?

Round 2
Italian composer or pasta?
For the next five questions, I will give you a word, and you have to tell me if it is the name of an Italian composer or the name of a type of pasta.

Q6. CIVIDALE

Q7. PESENTI

Q8. BIGOLI

Q9. SAGNARELLI

Q10. DENTICE

Round 3
Bald people, then and now

All you have to do is name these people who are now all hairless.

Q11.

Q12.

Q13.

Q14.

Q15.

Round 4
The BEIGE round

I have replaced colours in the following titles of songs, books and films. For example, if the question were FIFTY SHADES OF BEIGE, you would instantly recognise the title.

Your job is to tell me what the proper titles are.

Q16. BEIGE IS THE NEW BEIGE (book and TV)

Q17. THE COLOR BEIGE (book and film)

Q18. BEIGE AND CLOVER (song by Tommy James and the Shondells)

Q19. BEIGE TEETH (book)

Q20. This last one is the first two lines of a famous song. Give me the song title (which does not contain a colour).

BEIGE AND BEIGE AND BEIGE AND BEIGE
BEIGE AND BEIGE AND BEIGE

Round 5
Famous sporting feet

To whom do these feet belong? For Q23, I want the owner of the socked feet in the middle.

Q21.   Q22.   Q23.

Q24.   Q25.

Round 6
Connections

Q26. What connects the words PETTY, HOLLAND and FORD?

Q27. What famous chef received a large windfall in 2022 despite his chain of restaurants collapsing with millions owed to suppliers?

Q28. One of the most successful Swiss football teams is called the YOUNG ___ what?

Q29. What was the name of the central character created by the vicar Wilbert Awdry?

Q30. What dessert do you get if you fold fruit into sweet custard?

Q31. What is the first name of the famous Polish footballer Lewandowski?

Q32. So, what's the connection?

QUIZ No. 12

Round 1
Brainteasers

Q1. Anne's mother has five children. Four are called Brian, Charlotte, Delia and Edward. What is the name of the fifth child?

Q2. Martha buys a bottle of wine and a bag to put it in, all for £11. The bottle of wine costs £10 more than the bag. How much does the bag cost?

Q3. A taxi driver left the house but forgot to take his driver's licence with him. He went the wrong way down a one-way street. A traffic police officer witnessed him do this but took no action. Why?

Q4. Seven sisters are at home, each busy with something: Anabel is reading a book; Belinda is preparing some food; Cherrie is playing chess; Dora is playing Candycrush on her phone; Eleanor is working out a Sudoku puzzle; Fran is watering the plants on the windowsill. So, what is the seventh sister, Gladys, doing?

Q5. A man pushes his car to a hotel and tells the owner he's bankrupt. Why?

Round 2
First or Last

Q6. In the 1992 film, Daniel Day-Lewis played the last what?

Q7. The Russian Valentina Tereshkova was the first woman to do what?

Q8. In 1875, Captain Matthew Webb was the first to achieve what sporting feat?

Q9. Name the first actor or actress to appear on a postage stamp

Q10. Lady Louise Mountbatten-Windsor is whose first child?

Round 3
Maps and landmarks

Q11. What tall building is located at the indicated point south of the Thames?

Q12. What very large building is located at the cross on the map?

Q13. Name both the large land masses on this map.

Q14. The tall building marked by the dot in the top right contains the city's name and a number that represents the number of floors in the building. Name the building.

Q15. What is the name of the famous bridge in the city marked on this map?

Round 4
Songs from film and tv

Q16. The Rembrandts perform a song called *I'll be there for you*. It is the theme tune to what long-running TV comedy?

Q17. Ennio Morricone's *Ecstasy of Gold* accompanies the end scene of a famous film. This scene is set in a graveyard. Name the film.

Q18. What song did George Peppard listen to Audrey Hepburn sing on her window sill?

Q19. The only song Louis Armstrong performed for a James Bond film was called *We have all the time in the world*. What was the Bond film in question?

Q20. The song called *The Unknown Stuntman* was the theme song to what TV series?

Round 5
Things you can find around the house, in close-up
Name these items

Q21.

Q22.

Q23.

Q24.

Q25. This one is
more usually found
in the pub

Round 6
Connections
Q26. An easy one to start with. What famous singer has had two partners, one called Bianca and the other called Jerry?

Q27. What was the first name of the famous actor who died while filming *Gladiator*?

Q28. Name the 2008 comedy film starring Owen Wilson and Jennifer Aniston about a couple whose life changes when they adopt a free-spirited pup who, along with his antics, manages to teach them and their children important life lessons.

Q29. Name the famous magician and illusionist once married to the supermodel Claudia Schiffer.

Q30. What word is something you find in an apple and something that marks the time on the radio?

Q31. The baseball team in Los Angeles is called the LA what?

Q32. So, what's the connection?

QUIZ No. 13

Round 1
Words and spelling
Q1. What is the difference between STATIONERY and STATIONARY?
Q2. What is KOHLRABI?
Q3. BAIKONUR is a place that serves a particular function. What is that function?
Q4. What artificial material was the lead singer of the punk band X-Ray Spex?
Q5. What word, most often associated with parliament and the legal profession, is given to the act of speaking at length to obstruct progress in reaching a decision or passing a new law?

Round 2
Words from the Periodic Table
I am spelling words using the symbols of elements. For example, if I asked you to spell a word made from Nitrogen+Oxygen+Selenium, you would spell N+O+Se = NOSE. All these answers are found in or are about the pub.
Q6. CARBON + OXYGEN + ACTINIUM + HYDROGEN
Q7. AMERICIUM + BORON + ERBIUM is a fossilised resin and a member of the pub's bar staff.
Q8. BERYLLIUM + ERBIUM
Q9. TANTALUM + NITROGEN + POTASSIUM + ARGON + DEUTERIUM
Q10. SILICON + MOLYBDENUM + NITROGEN

Round 3
Eyes down
Name these people from just their eyes.

Q11.  Q12.  Q13.

Q14.  Q15.

Round 4
Compass points
Q16. Which city is the furthest west: Bristol or Edinburgh?
Q17. Which UK city was home to Northern Soul's famous night club?
Q18. Which country has the northernmost border with Russia?
Q19. Which is more to the North: Buckingham Palace or the London Eye?
Q20. If you travel east from the Falkland Islands, which country do you hit first?

Round 5
Stills from music videos
Name the songs and the performers from these images

Q21.   Q22.

Q23.   Q24.

Q25.

Round 6

Connections

Q26. What household item, with an average head length of 20 to 30 mm, was first mass-produced in England in the 1700s by William Addis?

Q27. What word is a species of crab, a good luck charm and a game played by George Bush Snr at the White House?

Q28. If FILLETTE equals one half, CHAMPENOISE equals one, JEROBOAM equals four, and METHUSELAH equals eight, what word is used for two?

Q29. What am I talking about when I say 6H is the hardest and 8B is the softest?

Q30. What C is a traffic calming tool, a heraldic device or an indication of rank?

Q31. In Lewis Carroll's poem, who says the following lines before eating lots of oysters:

      'The time has come,' the _____ said,

      'To talk of many things:

      Of shoes—and ships—and sealing-wax—

      Of cabbages—and kings—

      And why the sea is boiling hot—

      And whether pigs have wings.'

Q32. So, what's the connection?

QUIZ No. 14

Round 1
General Knowledge
Q1. Name the actor who won an Oscar for playing the scientist Stephen Hawking.
Q2. The palatine glands are more commonly known as what?
Q3. What do the artist Munch, the composer Grieg and the playwright Ibsen all have in common, apart from each having five letters in their surnames?
Q4. In England, whose official salary is about 6,000 pounds and a barrel of sherry?
Q5. Unless they are touring the world, two of this document's four known surviving copies are housed in the British Library in London, one at Salisbury Cathedral and one at Lincoln Castle. What is this document?

Round 2
Cities and city districts that have given their name to something
Q6. The 1957 Treaty of Rome established what?
Q7. The Manhattan Project focused on the development of what?
Q8. What one word is a London district, a board game and a brand of computer accessories?
Q9. What city gave its name to an emotional response when hostage victims have positive feelings toward their captor?
Q10. The song Take My Breath Away featured in the film Top Gun. The performer is the name of a city. Name the city.

Round 3
Dogs in the movies
Name these five dogs.

Q11.    Q12.   Q13.

 Q14.  Q15.

Round 4
Sporting nationalities
Q16. Romelu Lukaku plays for which international team?

Q17. Ashleigh Barty, the Australian Open champion in 2022, holds what nationality?

Q18. Mondo Duplantis is the current world record holder in the pole vault. He holds dual nationality with the USA, but what country does he represent in international competition?

Q19. Kane Williamson is the current captain of which country's test cricket team?

Q20. Charles LeClerc is a Formula One driver for Ferrari. What country does he call home?

Round 5
Things that grow
Name these five things that grow.

 Q21.  Q22.

Q23. Q24.

Q25.

Round 6
Connections
Q26. Which Swiss football team shares its name with an insect?

Q27. Who wrote *Cat on a Hot Tin Roof*?

Q28. What actor has played the title role in *Black Widow*, *The Other Boleyn Girl* and *Girl With A Pearl Earring*?

Q29. What word is the diminutive of the Spanish word for 'war' and means 'member of a small independent group, usually fighting larger forces'?

Q30. In the advert for a men's cologne, a man drives a car past a bison, gets a shovel and buries his jewellery in the sand. Either deep and meaningful or utter tosh, but who is the man in that advert?

Q31. In the Disney film *Pocahontas*, what animal is Meeko?

Q32. So, what's the connection?

QUIZ No. 15
Valentine's Day Special

Round 1
Romantic general knowledge
Q1. According to *The Gentleman's Journal*, only one seafood makes it onto the Top Ten best aphrodisiacs. What is it?

Q2. In May 2010, Paris expressed concern over the growing number of what on its bridges? In 2014, part of one footbridge even fell into the Seine.

Q3. We associate the heart with romance. The heart is made up of four chambers. Two on the right and two on the left. What are they called? (two answers – half a point for each)

Q4. Roses, chocolates and, of course, champagne usually accompany Valentine's Day. What was the name of the Benedictine monk who invented champagne?

Q5. Interflora's logo features the Roman god of messengers, translators and interpreters. In the logo, he is carrying a bunch of flowers. What is that Roman god's name?

Round 2
Valentine's music round
All the song titles in this round contain the word LOVE

Q6. This is the first verse of a famous song. What is it called?

> 'Sometimes I feel I've got to
> Run away I've got to
> Get away
> From the pain you drive into the heart of me
> The love we share
> Seems to go nowhere
> And I've lost my light
> For I toss and turn, I can't sleep at night.'

Q7. According to the UK charts, what is the best-selling song of all time with the word LOVE in the title? It spent 15 weeks at No.1 and features on the soundtrack of a famous romantic film.

Q8. Name the song that features this cheesy spoken section.
  'And though my friends just might ask me
  They say, "Martin, maybe one day you'll find true love"
  I say, "Maybe there must be a solution
  To the one thing, the one thing we can't find."'
Q9. In his biggest hit, Tom Odell sings about what kind of love?
Q10. Name the song with the fabulous lyrics from the final verse:
  'The final chapter – prophetic, poetic
  When I'm done, this calls for anaesthetic.'

Round 3
Back-to-back romcom posters
Name the films from these almost-all back-to-back posters.

Q11.　　　　Q12.　　　　　　　　Q13.

Q14.　　　　Q15.

Round 4
Valentine Round
All these questions feature VALENTINE either in the question or in the answer.
Q16. Which Shakespeare play features a bloke called Valentine and a bloke called Proteus?
Q17. Which film stars Pauline Collins as a disillusioned housewife who travels on a package holiday?

Q18. MESSY ADRENALIN CAVEATS is an anagram of what event on this day in history?

Q19. Which Frank Sinatra song features the following lyrics:

'You make me smile with my heart
Your looks are laughable
Unphotographable
Yet you're my favourite work of art.'

Q20. As well as being the unofficial patron saint of love, of what occupation is St Valentine also believed to be the patron?

Round 5
Romantic films

Q21. What romcom features the famous line, 'I'm just a girl, standing in front of a boy, asking him to love her'?

Q22. You may well have watched Colin Firth and Jennifer Erhle in the BBC's adaptation of the terribly romantic *Pride and Prejudice*. Those two actors have also appeared in an Oscar-winning film. What is that film called?

Q23. What is the name of the 1954 romcom starring Humphrey Bogart and Audrey Hepburn, which was remade in 1995 with Harrison Ford and Julia Ormond?

Q24. What famous novel, adapted into a romantic film, contains the line, 'I've come here with no expectations, only to profess, now that I am at liberty to do so, that my heart is, and always will be, yours.'

Q25. And what about this film that features the following line near the end, 'When you realize you want to spend the rest of your life with somebody, you want the rest of your life to start as soon as possible.'

Round 6
Connections and, yes, it's romantic

Q26. This is a world-famous art museum. What is it called?

Q27. Name the beauty on the left. Clue: the bloke on the right was played in film by Brad Pitt

Q28. Which West End musical begins with an auction scene where this monkey music box is sold?

Q29. What is this foodie film called?

Q30. For what is this the official logo?

Q31. Here is a famous monologue.
Name the film where it appears:
'I don't know who you are. I don't
know what you want. If you are
looking for ransom, I can tell you I
don't have money, but what I do
have are a very particular set of
skills. Skills I have acquired over a
very long career. Skills that make
me a nightmare for people like
you. If you let my daughter go now,
that'll be the end of it. I will not
look for you, I will not pursue you,
but if you don't, I will look for you, I
will find you, and I will kill you.'

Q32. So, what's the connection?

QUIZ No. 16

Round 1
A mixed bag with numbers in the questions or answers
Q1. Steve Martin, Chevy Chase and Martin Short starred in a comedy film with a number in the title. What is the title of that film?
Q2. What product is classified in Italy as 00, 0, 1 and 2, in France as 45, 55, 80 and 110, while the UK has no numbered system of classification?
Q3. In one movie, Arnold Schwarzenegger says two words from a truck. In the sequel to this movie, Robert Patrick says the same two words, only from a helicopter. What are those two words?
Q4. Who had the prisoner number 24601?
Q5. The last in this round is a royalty question. King Edward I had been married to Eleanor of Castile for 36 years. While on a royal visit, she died near Lincoln in the year 1290. It took 12 nights to return to London, and the king ordered a monument to be erected in his wife's memory at each stop. Where in London is the last of these famous monuments?

Round 2
The Matt round
This is a special round, as our friend Matt flew all the way in from Texas to play. Sort of. I couldn't let that dedication go unrewarded, so I have devised a round, especially for Matt or Matthew, whatever you prefer to call yourself.
Q6. Matthew the Apostle was one of Jesus's twelve disciples. What was his occupation?
Q7. There is a Matt AND a Matthew among the six actors who play leading roles in the sitcom Friends. Name both their surnames for the point.
Q8. What is the surname of Matt, who created the Simpsons?
Q9. Luke and Matt are two brothers who comprise which pop singing duo?
Q10. Which Matthew starred in *Ferris Bueller's Day Off*?

Round 3
People when young
Can you name these five famous faces from photos in their youth?

Q11.   Q12.

Q13.   Q14.   Q15.

Round 4
Winter Olympics
Q16. Which Olympic sport is played on a surface that is a sheet ice is over 45 metres long and a maximum of five metres wide?
Q17. Cool Runnings is a film about the exploits of a bobsleigh team from which country?
Q18. The Winter Olympics have just closed. Which country topped the medal table this time?
Q19. In what sport do competitors convert potential energy into kinetic energy to cover the greatest distance in K-98 or K-125 disciplines?
Q20. Axel Paulsen, Ulrich Salchow and Alois Lutz competed in what sport?

Round 5
Iconic women

Q21. This woman wrote her most famous work of literature when she was 19. Who was she?

Q22. Gabrielle Bonheur are whose birth-given first names?

Q23. Who is this below?

Q24. This woman on the right declared that 'One is not born but becomes a woman', a statement that continues to reverberate in contemporary discussions of gender. Who is she?

Q25. This is Junko Tabei. She was the first woman to do what?

Round 6
Connections
Q26. Hydrophobia is another name for what disease?
Q27. What kind of MAN won Best Picture Oscar in 1989?
Q28. What word means to smooth the surface of wood, the name of the tool that performs this action, a tall tree with bark that peels unevenly and a fixed-wing aircraft?

Q29. Jude Law plays a Soviet sniper in a film called WHAT at the Gates?

Q30. What type of gang did the Pretenders sing about in their 1982 single?

Q31. Lynyrd Skynyrd, Dolly Parton and Hear-Say all released songs called *WHAT and Simple*?

Q32. So, what's the connection?

QUIZ No. 17

Round 1
Geographical mixed bag
Q1. What is the only country in the world to have a picture of the country on its flag?
Q2. What is the name of the lake where Germany, Switzerland and Austria all meet?
Q3. What is the capital city of the largest country in Africa?
Q4. Name the river that flows through Albuquerque, El Paso and Brownsville.
Q5. Alcatraz was an island prison just over a mile away from which major city?

Round 2
Is it a racehorse, or is it a drag queen?
All you have to tell me for each answer is to what each name refers: a racehorse or a drag queen from *Ru Paul's Drag Race*.
Q6. Magnolia Crawford
Q7. Rachel Alexandra
Q8. Scarlet Envy
Q9. Jewel Princess
Q10. Ginger Punch

Round 3
Sitcom interiors
Name the sitcom from these empty interiors.

Q11.  Q12.

Q13.  Q14.

Q15.

Round 4
The Three Musketeers
Q16. Who wrote *The Three Musketeers*?

Q17. Aramis and Porthos were two of the three Musketeers. Who was the other?

Q18. What was the name of the evil cardinal, adviser to the King and allegedly the most powerful man of the time?

Q19. The author of the novel wrote a sequel to *The Three Musketeers*, also known as *The D'Artagnan Romances*. It is called ___ *Years After*. What is the missing number?

Q20. There is a canine version of *The Three Musketeers*, originally a Spanish-Japanese cartoon. It was released as a CGI feature last year, too. Give me the full title of that ridiculous pun-filled canine animated film.

Round 5
Musical instruments
Name these instruments.

Q21. Q22. Q23.

Q24. Q25.

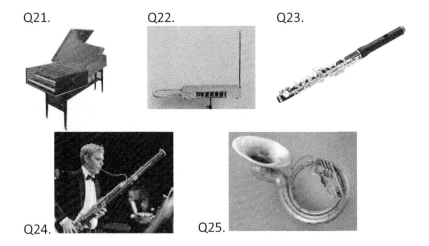

Round 6
Connections

Q26. What is the surname of the actor who played the villain in the last James Bond film *No Time To Die* and Freddie Mercury in the film *Bohemian Rhapsody*?

Q27. What is the 6-letter shortened name of the longest-running soap opera on television?

Q28. Which English town in the West Midlands shares its name with the first name of the comedy actor who starred in the films *Arthur* and *Bedazzled*?

Q29. What is the first name of the French female athlete Barber, who was the World Heptathlon champion in 1999, the world long jump champion in 2003, and who was found guilty of resisting arrest in an alleged racially-motivated persecution in 2008?

Q30. What is the surname of the American President who appears on the $100 bill?

Q31. What is the first name of the singer, nicknamed the Empress of Soul, whose most famous song is Midnight Train To Georgia?

Q32. So, what's the connection?

QUIZ No. 18

Round 1
Coincidences
Q1. Name the writer who was born on the day Halley's Comet appeared in the sky in 1835 and died on the day it next appeared, which was in 1910. He is most famous for writing stories about a young lad who grew up on the Mississippi River. He famously predicted his death by saying, 'The Almighty has said, no doubt, 'Now here are these two unaccountable freaks; they came in together, they must go out together.'

Q2. In a Simpsons episode of the year 2000, what event did the cartoon accurately predict would happen?

Q3. This person was assassinated while travelling in a car with the number plate A 111 118, the same date (11/11/18) as Armistice Day. Who was he?

Q4. Which famous actor, who died in 1984, starred in a film version of 1984, which was made in 1984?

Q5. Two men, whose full names each contain 15 letters, each allegedly assassinated a prominent person whose surnames each contain seven letters. The first man committed the assassination in a theatre and was caught in a warehouse. The second man committed the assassination from a warehouse and was caught in a theatre. Name the two prominent people who were assassinated.

Round 2
Detectives
Q6. What literary character lives in the village of St Mary Mead?

Q7. What famous detective is the creation of the writer Georges Simenon?

Q8. Name the famous detective who lived in a trailer and drove a golden brown Pontiac Firebird.

Q9. In *Hawaii Five-O*, what is Detective Steve McGarrett's most famous catchphrase?

70

Q10. Douglas Adams is most famous for his *Hitchhiker's Guide to the Galaxy*, but he also created a time-travelling detective. What was his name?

Round 3
Famous gates
Name these gates.

Q11.

Q12.

Q13.

Q14.

Q15.

Round 4
Best Picture Oscars round
Q16. Which famous Best Picture Oscar winner tells the story of a selfish LA yuppie who learns his estranged father has left a fortune to an autistic brother in Ohio who he didn't know existed?
Q17. Two films starring Russell Crowe won Best Picture at the Oscars in two successive years. *Gladiator* was one. What was the other?
Q18. Which Best Picture Oscar about greed and class discrimination was the first foreign-language film to win the award?
Q19. Which Best Picture from the Oscars asked questions about the cricketer with the most first-class centuries and the name of the man who invented the first commercially successful revolver?
Q20. The popular website IMDB, which rates the best-ever films based on viewer votes, has consistently had *The Shawshank Redemption* at Number One. However, that great film was beaten to the Best Picture Oscar by a Tom Hanks film. What film was that?

Round 5
Famous spouses
Don't tell me who these people are; tell me who their famous spouses are.

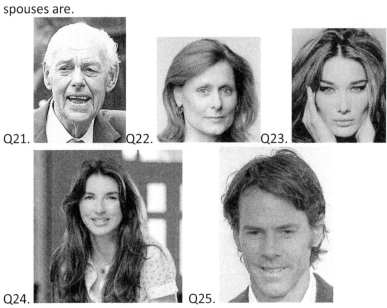

Q21. Q22. Q23.

Q24. Q25.

Round 6
Connections
Q26. What profession requires workers to pass a test called 'The Knowledge'?
Q27. PETER, SUSAN and EDMUND are three children from the Chronicles of Narnia series of books. Who is the fourth child?
Q28. What is the first name of the boxer who defeated Muhammad Ali to win the undisputed heavyweight championship in 1978?
Q29. Which fast-food chain has more outlets than any other in the world?
Q30. What is the Japanese word for 'Divine Wind'?
Q31. What is missing from this sequence?
1. HYDROGEN 2. HELIUM 3. LITHIUM 4. BERYLLIUM 6. CARBON
Q32. So, what's the connection?

QUIZ No. 19

Round 1
Sequences of four
Q1. Give me the odd one out from the following four words.
QUEEN—MERCHANT—WIVES—KING
Q2. What do the cities York (England), Dubrovnik (Croatia), Quebec City (Canada) and Obidos (Portugal) all have in common?
Q3. Insert the missing word:
POLAND – KRAKOWIAK
AFGHANISTAN – PAKOL
SOUTH AFRICA – ISICHOLO
MEXICO -?
Q4. What comes next in this sequence: King's Cross, Fenchurch Street, Liverpool Street _____?
Q5. BLOODY, SALT, WAKEFIELD and WHITE are all structures you can find in a particular place in London. What are they?

Round 2
Famous films as they are translated into different languages
In my work as a translator, I often find that things acquire new meaning when put into Russian, sometimes with ridiculous consequences. Take, for example, the film *The Shawshank Redemption*. The Russian translation generously inserts a massive spoiler into the title, for it is called *Escape from Shawshank Prison*. Magic. Here are the titles of films as they appear in different countries. Your job is to tell me by what name we know these films.
Q6. The Young People Who Traverse Dimensions While Wearing Sunglasses (as it is known in France)
Q7. Vaseline (as it is known in Argentina)
Q8. Mom, I Missed the Plane (as it is known in France)
Q9. It's Raining Falafel (as it is known in Israel)
Q10. And last but not least, the most apt title of them all:
Meetings And Failures In Meetings (as it is known in Portugal)

Round 3
Sweet stuff
Name these sweet treats

  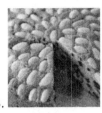

Q11. Q12. Q13.

Q14. This is Amelie, whose favourite sound is produced with a spoon. What is her favourite dessert?

Q15. Finally, what is this?

Round 4
Riddles
Q16. I have a head. I have a tail. I have no body. What am I?
Q17. Tall when young. Short when old. What am I?
Q18. I shave every day, but my beard gets no shorter. What am I?
Q19. What travels all over the world but sits in the corner?
Q20. I am a word that begins with the letter I. If you add the letter A to me, I become a new word with a different meaning, but that sounds the same. What word am I?

Round 5
MEMES

Q21. This meme of John Travolta is often used when there is nothing to be found. From which film was this image taken?

Q22. Who is this, used for a self-explanatory meme?

Going to work

Going to work to pick up my paycheck

Q23. This popular meme for congratulating someone is taken from which film?

Q24. Here is a message of wisdom, but in which sitcom does this character appear?

Q25. 'Boss: Are you ready to come back to the office?
Me: Not even close, not even a little bit, not even at all.'
A meme with these words accompanies this image of Julia Stiles, but from which film?

Round 6

Connections

Q26. Arnold Schwarzenegger starred in the film *Twins* with which other actor?

Q27. What did Liza tell Henry to fix in the children's nursery rhyme?

Q28. At 280/180 mmHg, what creature has the highest blood pressure?

Q29. NaCl is the chemical formula for what everyday item?

Q30. What is the surname of the family in *Only Fools and Horses*?

Q31. What is the first name of the girl who cried at the discotheque after a murder on the dancefloor?

Q32. So, what's the connection?

QUIZ No. 20

Round 1
This week's news
(Monday 21 March 2022)
Q1. The feast of which saint was celebrated last Thursday?
Q2. There have been debates on both sides of the Pond this month about doing away with the process of changing the clocks forward and backwards. What is this process called in the United States?
Q3. This month hasn't been great for seagulls. A bloke in Plymouth threw one at another man in a fight and broke his jaw with it, while another was plucked from the air and killed by a creature at Chester Zoo. What creature?
Q4. Nazanin Zaghari-Ratcliffe returned to the UK after six years in an Iranian prison. She was greeted at the airport by her husband, Richard and 7-year-old daughter. What is the daughter's name?
Q5. In a new book by royal biographer Robert Hardman, published this week, it is revealed that former Labour minister Alan Johnson, during a visit to Buckingham Palace, accidentally ate biscuits that were not for him. Can you guess who they were for?

Round 2
Collectors
Q6. What does a LEPIDOPTERIST collect?
Q7. What does a PHILOGRAPHIST collect?
Q8. A TEGESTOLOGIST might often be found in drinking establishments. What do they collect?
Q9. What do you call someone who collects coins, banknotes and medals?
Q10. HELIXOPHILES are probably the most popular party guests. What do they collect?

Round 3
Sporting trophies

Q11. This trophy is the smallest in world sport and yet the most coveted in the sport for which it is awarded. What is the trophy called?

Q12. For which world championship is this the prize? Yes, thank you, tattoo-armed person, for pointing to it for us.

Q13. With snakes for handles and an elephant on the top, what is this trophy called?

Q14. That is Ronald Coeman if you're interested. What is the name of the trophy he is holding?

Q15. Here is a section of a famous sporting trophy. What is it called (the trophy, not the tournament)?

Round 4
Classic last lines from films
Here are some famous lines. From what films are they taken?
Q16. I think this is the beginning of a beautiful friendship.
Q17. I do wish we could chat longer, but I'm having an old friend for dinner.
Q18. The greatest trick the devil ever pulled was convincing the world he did not exist. And like that... he is gone.
Q19. All right, Mr DeMille, I'm ready for my close-up.
Q20. In case I don't see you, good afternoon, good evening, and goodnight.

Round 5
Famous people endorsing products

Q21. What is Elton John advertising here?

Q22. Ozzy Osborne is looking a little confused. What is he advertising?

Q23. Who's the handsome chap in the tanktop advertising Chesterfield cigarettes?

Q24. What is Snoop Dogg advertising here?

Q25. An old classic, this one. What is the product being advertised?

Round 6
Connections
Q26. At 73 miles long, what runs from Newcastle to Solway Firth via Carlisle?

Q27. What is the real name of George Alan O'Dowd?

Q28. What do Catherine the Great, King Wenceslas III of Bohemia, Vincent Vega and Elvis Presley all have in common?

Q29. Myelopathy, Kyphosis and Radiculopathy are afflictions of what?

Q30. In cricket, what is the name of the distance of 22 yards between wickets?

Q31. What colour is the creator of Robert Langdon or the lead singer of the Stone Roses?

Q32. So, what's the connection?

QUIZ No. 21

Round 1
Big business

Q1. Jeff Bezos was overtaken by another ridiculously wealthy person who, among other things, owns a famous car brand. What is that car brand?

Q2. You might not know this, but Jared Leto and Snoop Dogg are partial owners of a well-known social media platform whose logo is a smiling alien head with a single antenna on top. What is that platform called?

Q3. In recent years, Mike Ashley's Sports Direct has purchased numerous struggling companies. One has a kangaroo logo. What is the brand?

Q4. The RR McReynolds Company recently took over which football club?

Q5. Longines, Tissot, Omega and Rado are four of the brands owned by the world's largest watch business. What is that watch business called?

Round 2
The Sean round

Sean is a regular player in the pub, and this round marks his first-ever quiz. This round is all about Seans, how ever you care to spell the name.

Q6. Which film, directed by Edgar Wright and starring Simon Pegg and Nick Frost, features the name Shaun

Q7. What Sean famously advertises Yorkshire Tea while brandishing a sword?

Q8. In what film does Sean Connery play John Mason, the only man ever reported to have escaped from Alcatraz?

Q9. What famous Shaun has friends who include Bitzer the dog, Pidsley the cat and the Naughty Pigs.

Q10. What is the name of the short drama series recently aired on TV, where Sean Bean plays a prisoner and Stephen Graham, the prison officer?

Round 3
Maps

Q11. This is a map of whose famous travels?

Q12. Who first completed this flight route?

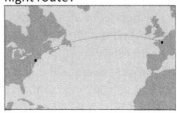

Q13. How long did this journey take?

Q14. What is the name of the dark line on this map of the east coast of America, which Mark Knopfler and James Taylor famously sang about?

Q15. Which sportsman's route map is this?

Round 4
Songs containing countries
Q16. David Bowie sang about what kind of girl? Give me the title of the song.

Q17. The Human League sang about a country that has a Mediterranean coastline. What is that country?

Q18. Which Kirsty MacColl song begins with the line 'I was twenty-one years when I wrote this song'?

Q19. A British island territory in the North Atlantic Ocean features in a Barry Manilow song. What's the song called?

Q20. Childish Gambino sang a song called *This is _____*. What country is the missing word?

Round 5

Just name the cartoon characters whose heads I have replaced with cardoon flowers.

Q21.   Q22.   Q23.

Q24.   Q25.

Round 6
Connections

Q26. If I pour advocaat and lemonade over ice with lime juice, what do I get?

Q27. Sidney Poitier played the role of what police character in the Oscar-winning film In *The Heat of the Night*?

Q28. What was the title of Camilla before she became Queen Consort?

Q29. X arrives at the yard, smelling fresh paint. He asks Henry what the painters are working on, and Henry tells him that James is getting a new coat. What is the full name of X in this story?

Q30. What is the first name of the national security adviser who shredded documents in the Iran-contra arms-for-hostages scandal?

Q31. What famous comic tale, put to a Mozart opera, relates how two servants succeed in tying the knot, foiling the efforts of their employer, Count Almaviva, seducing the female servant, and teaching him a lesson in fidelity?

Q32. So, what's the connection?

QUIZ No. 22
Mother's Day Special

Round 1
General mother-based trivia
Q1. What is affectionately known as 'mother's ruin'?
Q2. What, according to the proverb, is the 'mother of all invention'?
Q3. A famous woman question for you now. To what did Mary Anne Evans change her name in a bid to have her writing taken seriously?
Q4. This French female tennis player is affectionately known as 'The Mother of French Tennis'. She died in 1938 and won six Wimbledon singles titles. A court at the French Open bears her name. Who was she?
Q5. Teresa would visit her son in prison and bring him a large plate of macaroni, tomatoes and cheese on every visit. She could not speak much English, and when her son was transferred to the Atlanta Penitentiary, where foreign languages were not permitted, she could be heard to mutter that her son was 'a good boy'. Who was her son?

Round 2
Mother's Day traditions
Q6. What is the name of the rich fruit cake decorated with marzipan, which is traditionally associated with both Easter and Mother's Day?
Q7. In what country do people worship the Mother Goddess Durga?
Q8. In the Soviet Union, mothers were awarded a medal called Heroine Mother if they gave birth to how many children or more?
Q9. To remember Mothering Sunday in the UK it always falls on the fourth Sunday of what religious event?
Q10. In the UK, we call Mother's Day 'Mothering Sunday', which is actually a day where we honour our mother churches, the churches where what has happened?

Round 3

Flowers

Traditionally, we all love sending our mothers and loved ones flowers, but how many of these blooms can you name?

Q11. Name this flower

Q12. Name this flower

Q13. What popular flower is this?

Q14. Another flower image. Name that flower

Q15. Here's a film poster. Well, part of one; I'm not going to give you the answer.
The film's title contains a flower. Give me that film title (in full, please)

Round 4

Sporting mothers

Q16. What famous mother holds the world women's marathon record? She won the New York Marathon in 2007, just nine months after the birth of her daughter.

Q17. Oracene Price is the mother of two incredibly successful sporting sisters. Who are they?

Q18. What famous mother competed in equestrian sport at the 1976 Olympics in Montreal? Her daughter followed in her footsteps and represented Great Britain at the 2012 London Olympics.

Q19. Who won the 2009 US Open tennis championship in what was called 'The Mother of All Comebacks'. It came just 16 months after giving birth to her daughter.

Q20. Florence Griffith Joyner and Gail Devers were medal-winning American athletes in the 1980s. However, they are perhaps best known for the impressive length of... what?

Round 5
Famous mothers

Q21. Name the mother of the pictured offspring

Q22. In this picture, a mother is presenting her daughter with an award. Name the recipient.

Q23. I reckon this mother looks rather like her son, who is obscured on the right. Who is the son?

Q24. Here is a picture of mother and child, with the child's face obscured. Give me the child's name.

Q25. Wow, this mother really does look like her son. Who is the son?

Round 6
Connections to suit the occasion

Q26. What fictional character has a mother called Zinnia, a father called Harry and a teacher called Miss Honey?

Q27. What is the first name of the mother in The Waltons, played by Michael Learned?

Q28. What is the name of the Albanian-Indian Roman Catholic nun and missionary who died in 1997 and was canonised in 2016?

Q29. What is the surname of the artist who produced a controversial piece called *Mother and Child. Divided*? It was controversial because it featured a cow and a calf severed in half.

Q30. Which monarch succeeded the last monarch of the House of Hanover and preceded the first monarch of the House of Windsor?

Q31. What is the one-word title of the Netflix original film that was nominated for 10 Oscars in 2018 and won 3, including best foreign language film? It centres around a mother, her children and their two maids.

Q32. So, what is the connection?

QUIZ No. 23

Round 1
In the news
(11 April 2022)
Q1. What famous sports star planned to play at the US Masters golf tournament after a road accident nearly meant he'd lose a leg?
Q2. Who last week announced he had acquired a 9.2% stake in the social media giant Twitter? Of course, he has since become the owner and has changed the platform's name.
Q3. The British Pop Archive exhibit is to open next week. In which British city?
Q4. As of this week, menus in restaurants owned by companies with more than 250 staff must print what on all their menus?
Q5. Officials at a town council in Cornwall cut down 1000 daffodils from a children's play park in a decision locals have called 'bonkers'. What was the reason they cut down the flowers?

Round 2
Towns and cities in film titles
Q6. Nicholas Cage won an Oscar for leaving what city?
Q7. Kevin Costner stars in a baseball film that features the name of a British city in its title. What is the name of that film?
Q8. Michael Caine stars in a spy film based on the book of the same name by Len Deighton. It contains the name of a major European capital city. What is the name of that film?
Q9. Which Sacha Baron Cohen film shares its name with a British town?
Q10. Matthew McConaughey won an Oscar in 2013 for his role in a film that contains an American city in the title. Name that film.

Round 3
Country outlines that look like other things

Q11. This country outline can be turned into a cute little doggy. Name the country.

Q12. With the addition of a couple of lines, whiskers into the Black Sea and a good dose of imagination, this country's outline looks like a little cat. Name the country.

Q13. This country outline looks like the arm of a swimmer. Honestly. Name the country.

Q14. This country looks like a seahorse. Name it.

Q15. This one looks a bit like a rhino head, which is an odd coincidence because this is one of the few countries where you can still find them in the wild. Name the country.

Round 4
The Latin round
This is a round about Latin phrases we have all heard of.

Q16. What famous rock band is the Latin for an existing state of affairs?

Q17. What is the name of a document written voluntarily under oath and used as evidence in court?

Q18. What is the English equivalent of the Latin term 'In flagrante delicto'?

Q19. What Latin term means repeating or continuing something to the point of boredom?

Q20. What is the Latin word for 'of sound mind' or 'in control of one's mind'?

Round 5
Famous faces defaced
I have played around with the Paint function on my computer, defacing images of famous people. All you have to do is name the famous people.

Q21. Q22. Q23.

Q24. Q25.

Round 6
Connections
Q26. What is the surname of the male footballer Alexis and the female tennis player Arantxa?

Q27. What one word goes before COUNTRY, SLEEP and FISH to make the name of a pop group, a work of literature and the title of a film?

Q28. G____ disease is an autoimmune disorder that causes an overactive thyroid. What is the G?

Q29. Which famous Humphrey Bogart film is set in the Florida Keys as a hurricane approaches?

Q30. In Cluedo, what ageing housekeeper character has been replaced by the biologist Dr Orchid?

Q31. What is the name of the Marvel Comics female superhero, a highly trained assassin who wields two swords, dresses in red and has been played in the movies by Jennifer Garner?

Q32. So, what's the connection?

QUIZ No. 24

Round 1
In the news
(18 April 2022)

Q1. The World Snooker Championships began at the weekend. What is the name of the venue that has hosted this tournament for the last 46 years?

Q2. What famous comedian and musician has the following formula for winning Eurovision? It states that 'If you're a music nerd, songs in the minor key usually win. Major key songs don't tend to win... the popular keys are G minor and D minor'.

Q3. In a Sunday Times list of the best places to live in the UK, which town came first in 2022?

Q4. The youngest-ever winner of this quiz show appeared in 2021, to be followed a year later by the oldest-ever winner. What is the quiz show?

Q5. In 2007, Liverpool was the first city outside London to host this. Other cities to follow suit have included Newcastle, Hull and Margate. In 2022, it was hosted in Liverpool again. What am I talking about?

Round 2
I give the answer; you give the question

Q6. 15 April 1912

Q7. 19 in 2008, 21 in 2011, 25 in 2015 and 30 in 2021

Q8. Sweden, with over 220,000

Q9. Gunther (151 episodes)

Q10. Belize (It has 12)

Round 3
The Bread Pitt round

Famous people transformed into food. Give their new names based on the food item. For example, this is a slice of bread featuring the face of Brad Pitt, making the answer Bread Pitt.

Q11.

Q12.

Q13.

Q14.

Q15.

Round 4
Famous people whose surnames contain cities

Q16. What famous footballer now co-hosts *Homes Under the Hammer*?

Q17. Which actor from *The Good Life* shares a surname with a town in the Lake District?

Q18. Name the actor who played the activists Steve Biko and Malcolm X

Q19. The Washington Monument stands at one end of a reflecting pool in Washington DC. A famous memorial building stands at the other end. To whom is that memorial building dedicated?

Q20. What comedian's real name was John Eric Bartholomew?

Round 5
Sites of famous battles
Name these battles from dots on maps.

Q21. Q22. Q23.

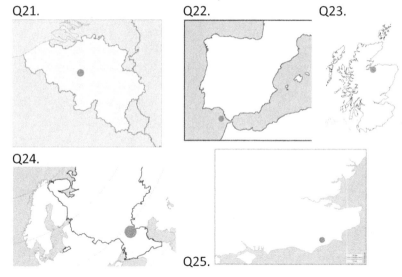

Q24.

Q25.

Round 6
Connections
Q26. What company was found primarily responsible for the disaster known by the name Deepwater Horizon?

Q27. What football team won the Premier League with the deadly strike partnership of Alan Shearer and Chris Sutton?

Q28. Trevor Francis was the first £1 million footballer. What team paid this record fee?

Q29. Anagram time. ARDENT LIMB is the anagram of which famous clothing brand that sounds just like a famous rapper and producer?

Q30. What fashion house began life as a maker of travel trunks and large suitcases? The logo features the interlocking initials of the designer.

Q31. What football team plays its home games at a stadium that has a bronze statue of Billy Bremner with arms aloft outside the entrance?

Q32. So, what's the connection?

QUIZ No. 25

Round 1
Famous streets
Q1. What television series is set on Ramsay Street?
Q2. On what street would you find one finger, two oranges, a strawberry and a triangle?
Q3. Who lived under the pillar-box outside 221C Baker Street, London?
Q4. On what street would you find The Kabin and Underworld?
Q5. The main street in what city is called Bourbon Street?

Round 2
People known by other names
These questions are all about people who have changed their names. I give you the name and even their year of birth and occupation. You have to tell me by what name they are better known.
Q6. Edson Arantes do Nascimento, born 1940 (sportsperson)
Q7. Lesley Hornby, born 1949 (model)
Q8. Shawn Corey Carter, born 1969 (musician)
Q9. Issur Danielovitch, born 1916 (actor)
Q10. Frances Ethel Gumm, born 1922 (actor)

Round 3
Famous people called Tony
Name these five

Q11. Q12. Q13.

Q14. Q15.

Round 4
Birds
Q16. What bird appears on the logo of the RSPB?
Q17. About what bird did Conchita Wurst sing in 2014?
Q18. What bird designed the monument to the Great Fire of London?
Q19. What is Europe's smallest bird?
Q20. In Mary Poppins, what can you make if you only have tuppence for paper and string?

Round 5
Dates in pretend Sun headlines
Look at these made-up Sun newspaper front pages and give me the year to which they refer. I will accept five years either way.

Q21. Q22. Q23.

Q24.

Q25.

Round 6
Connections

Q26. What was Midge Ure doing in 1984 with tears in his eyes?

Q27. Which region of the Czech Republic gives its name to the practice of leading an unconventional musical, literary, artistic or spiritual lifestyle?

Q28. An old car used to be parked at the MG plant in Abingdon, Oxfordshire, next to the factory's paint shop, which resulted in the vehicle becoming spattered in paint. To mark the 50th anniversary of the MG plant, a well-known brewery produced an ale, which it named after this car. Both MG and this beer have an octagonal logo. What is the name of the beer?

Q29. What was the name of the elusive character created by Baroness Orczy?

Q30. What word connects Europe's countdown, Warner Brothers' destination and Freddy Krueger's 1991 nightmare?

Q31. What is the name of the Hanna Barbera dog who is pale blue and wears a red bow tie and a straw boater?

Q32. So, what's the connection?

QUIZ No. 26

Round 1
Miscellaneous sport
Q1. Which snooker player matched Stephen Hendry's haul of seven world titles in 2022?
Q2. Who won the 2022 US Masters golf tournament?
Q3. What sport is played on the largest, fixed-size, rectangular pitch?
Q4. Which event in the decathlon involves the fastest speed?
Q5. Calvin Harrison won Gold at the 2000 Olympic Games in the 4x400m relay. Paul Hamm won Gold in the 2004 Olympic Games in the all-round gymnastics competition. Bob Bryan has won the most Grand Slam tennis doubles matches in history. These three sportsmen are all from the USA, but what else do they have in common?

Round 2
Cryptic song titles
Q6. What is this song's title?
CROSSING ACROSS TURBULENT H2O
Q7. Here's another song title. Can you name it from the cryptic clue?
COMPLETE DARKENING OF THE CORE
Q8. Name the following song that features four hand actions that are depicted in the following code
A TUNING FORK. THE GOLDEN ARCHES. A CRESCENT MOON. THE EIFFEL TOWER
Q9. What song title is this:
THINK ABOUT RELATIVES' WHEEL COVERING
Q10. IDOL + HARLOW makes up a famous Number One single by Michael Jackson. What is it?

Round 3
Reunions

Q11. This team reunited for an episode of Radio 4's *The Reunion*. What was their original show called?

Q12. How are these five collectively known? They are pictured here during their reunion tour.

Q13. What is the name of this band that performed a reunion tour in 2007?

Q14. Another band reunited for a single performance in 2013. What is this band called?

Q15. And finally for this round, we all know that Kate Winslett and Leonardo DiCaprio starred in *Titanic*, right? Well, they reunited to star in the film pictured here. What is that film called?

Round 4
Anagrams of famous people

Q16. HEADBANGER REGROWS is an anagram of what famous playwright?

Q17. HANGMAN ROTOR is an anagram of what talk show host?
Q18. JENNY, ATHENIAN BAUM is an anagram of what world leader?
Q19. HAM DIVED BACK is an anagram of what famous sportsperson?
Q20. PEASANTS DUG YUMA is an anagram of what famous figure of French literature?

Round 5
Snack logos
Name the snacks from these partial logos.

Q21. Q22. Q23.

Q24. Q25.

Round 6
Connections
Q26. What football team is the nearest point any team to ever come to achieving the quadruple (FA Cup, Carabao Cup, Champions League and Premiership)?
Q27. Who was BBC royal correspondent for 14 years before presenting *Cash in the Attic* and *Great British Menu*?
Q28. Which *Doctor Who* actor was the narrator of *Little Britain* sketches?
Q29. The Germans built Big Bertha for use in World War One. What was Big Bertha?
Q30. Who managed Frank Bruno, Joe Calzaghe, Ricky Hatton and Amir Khan, among other famous boxers.
Q31. What kind of boy was a film starring Josh Brolin and made in 2013? It is a remake of a classic 2003 Korean film of the same name.
Q32. So, what's the connection?

QUIZ No. 27

Round 1
Lead singers
1. Who is the lead singer of Coldplay?
2. Adam Levine is the lead singer of what band?
3. Who is the lead singer of The Killers?
4. Who was the lead singer of T. Rex?
5. Who is the lead singer of Talking Heads?

Round 2
Spelling Bee
Here are some simple questions. Your task? Spell the answers correctly.
6. What word is often written in the truncated form 'Misc.'?
7. What 8-letter word beginning with Q is a state of perplexity?
8. What 10-letter word beginning with D is a long-necked herbivorous dinosaur?
9. What type of shock is a severe, whole-body allergic reaction to a chemical that has become an allergen?
10. What P is an Italian type of sweet bread, originally from Milan, usually prepared and enjoyed for Christmas and the New Year?

Round 3
One-star film reviews
This round is all about film reviews, but not just any film reviews. These are one-star film reviews posted on Amazon by viewers. All you have to do is name the film being reviewed. I have not made these up; they are all genuine reviews.

★☆☆☆☆ **Cost me my marriage**
16 December 2017
Format: Prime Video

Terrifying, the very thought of toys coming alive when you aren't watching gave me chills. Subsequently I burned all my kids toys which apparently makes me a "bad father" and my wife has left me and taken the kids away from me. Terrible movie, ruined my life

Q11.

 Nate
★☆☆☆☆
May 11, 2019
Format: Prime Video

There was almost no blood in the whole movie.

Q12.

★☆☆☆☆ 2019 Los Angeles does not have flying cars, cloned people, nor off world colonies.

Q13.

★☆☆☆☆
September 21, 2018
Format: Prime Video

Maybe don't name your musical this if you don't even have a single song about leasing law, property management procedures, or net lease calculations. As a real estate professional I am very disappointed and feel I was misled.

★☆☆☆☆ **One Star**
By Joe Watson - December 14, 2014
There were no wolves in the movie.
0 of 3 people found this review helpful

Q14.   Q15.

Round 4
International car registration codes
All the answers are countries beginning with the letter B.
16. B
17. BH
18. BIH
19. BW
20. BS

Round 5
Famous people blended
Name both people for the point

Q21.   Q22.   Q23.

Q24.  Q25.

Round 6
Connections
Q26. Which former Royal Marine was the leader of the Liberal Democrats until 2009?

Q27. Name the one-word singer who sang the song with the following lyrics:

'Here I go out to sea again
The sunshine fills my hair
And dreams hang in the air
Gulls in the sky and in my blue eye
You know it feels unfair
There's magic everywhere.'

Q28. The singer and actor with the surname Martin and the actor with the first name James have the same respective other name. What is it?

Q29. When the pairing of Patrick Macnee and Diana Rigg later became the trio of Patrick Macnee, Joanna Lumley and Gareth Hunt, what word was added to the title?

Q30. What is the name of the 2007 Disney live animation film starring Amy Adams as Giselle, a dancing princess-to-be, and Susan Sarandon as the evil stepmother sorceress? The film is both a homage to and a self-parody of Disney's animated features, making numerous references to past films.

Q31. What kind of man won the Best Picture Oscar in 1988 and starred Tom Cruise?

Q32. So, what's the connection?

QUIZ No. 28

Round 1
Eurovision

Q1. When Ukraine won the Eurovision Song Contest in 2022, the UK came an incredible second. What is the name of the act that took second place?

Q2. Which country has the most Eurovision wins?

Q3. In 1973, the song *Ring Ring* failed in its bid to represent its country at Eurovision, although the same act won the following year. Name the act.

Q4. What country won the very first Eurovision Song Contest?

Q5. Which act won the Eurovision Song Contest for the UK in 1976? The song features a twist at the end where the singer is actually singing to his three-year-old-daughter.

Round 2
Military abbreviations

Q6. What type of military vehicle is an APC?

Q7. What type of weapon is an AAM?

Q8. If personnel in the armed forces are awarded a CGC, what do they receive?

Q9. Initially proposed by US President Ronald Reagan, for what does START stand?

Q10. Some military aircraft are given the term VTOL. For what does that stand?

Round 3
Cathedrals

Q11. What is the name of this famous gallery, famed for its unique acoustics?

Q12. This is the sanctuary knocker on the main entrance to which cathedral? In the 1980s, *Blue Peter* did a feature on its renovation, with the original and a replica displayed side by side. Simon Groom referred to them in his immortal children's television phrase: 'You must admit, they're a lovely pair of knockers'.

Q13. Here's a unique cathedral. In what capital city would you find it?

Q14. This is a plan of Canterbury Cathedral, typical of many British cathedrals in its layout. The dots mark parts of the cathedral that begin with the letter C. What does the dot with the arrow signify?

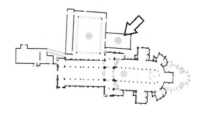

Q15. One of these three cathedrals is Chichester Cathedral. Which one?

A   B   C

Round 4
Odd-one-out
One point for telling me the odd-one-out, another for telling me why.
Q16. FEMUR – HUMERUS – RADIUS – ULNA
Q17. CHISWICK – BOSTON – GREEN – HOLLAND
Q18. EDGE – ELEMENT – ESCAPE – EXPLORER
Q19. CHITTY-CHITTY-BANG-BANG – KIDNAPPED – CASINO ROYALE – MOONRAKER
Q20. BISCUIT – BUNGALOW – SHAMPOO – JUGGERNAUT

Round 5
TV quiz shows
Q21. With what famous quiz show would you associate these outfits?

Q22. Name this show.

Q23. This is the logo for a more recent TV quiz show. What is it called?

108

Q24. This is Terry Wogan with his wand microphone. What show was he presenting here?

Q25. This is the new look for what long-running quiz show?

Round 6
Connections

Q26. Colin Firth played the artist Vermeer in what film?

Q27. This hero has a long nose and loves a woman called Roxanne. What is his name?

Q28. Complete the lyric, which is also the title of the song:
> 'Got to be what you wanna,
> If the groove don't get you, the rifle's gonna
> I'm serious as cancer when I say...'

Q29. What is the title of the song that features the following lines:
> 'Every single day
> Every word you say
> Every game you play
> Every night you stay'?

Q30. What capital city is made from a four-letter word for male facial hair and an English county?

Q31. Which film starring Matt Damon and Ben Affleck won an Oscar for best original screenplay, written by Matt Damon and Ben Affleck?

Q32. So, what's the connection?

QUIZ No. 29

Round 1
City names from nicknames
Q1. What city is known colloquially as *The Eternal City*?
Q2. What city is known as *The Big Easy*?
Q3. What city in Israel is known as *The Big Orange*?
Q4. What old walled city in Croatia is known as *The Pearl of the Adriatic*?
Q5. Which Yorkshire city is known as *The Wool City*? The Wool Exchange stands in the city centre.

Round 2
Tasting notes
These are tasting notes for a variety of drinks.
Q6. 'A medium-sweet white wine with refreshing stone fruit flavours. Goes with fruity desserts or on its own. A timeless classic German wine.'
Q7. 'It has a malty sweetness and a hoppy bitterness, with notes of coffee and chocolate. A roasted flavour also comes through, courtesy of the roasted unmalted barley that goes into its brewing. It has a sweet nose, with hints of malt breaking through, and its palate is smooth, creamy and balanced.'
Q8. 'A bubbling highland stream mixed with casual violence. But in a good way.'
Q9. What grape, most commonly appearing in an inexpensive student favourite, has the typical tasting note: 'pronounced acidity and fizz, medium tannin, sweet strawberry, cherry, rhubarb and violet'?
Q10. 'First produced in 1950 to commemorate Sir Winston Churchill's visit to Copenhagen, this lager has Cognac notes to reflect Churchill's favourite tipple. Blonde, with a sweet, bitter, nutty, caramel cognac-like flavour and a warming, rich, lingering finish.'

Round 3
Combined works of art
I have combined two famous works of art. Name both artists.

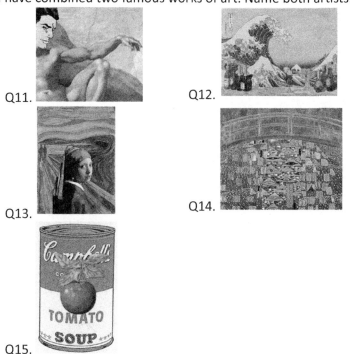

Q11.

Q12.

Q13.

Q14.

Q15.

Round 4
Ukrainian riddles
We hosted a Ukrainian family in 2002, and one of the daughters in the family, Kristina, told me some riddles for my quiz. You'll love these. Or not.

Q16. You enter a dark room in which there is a candle, a kerosene lamp and a gas stove. What do you light first?

Q17. With which hand is it best to stir the sugar in your tea?

Q18. What can you never eat for breakfast?

Q19. A dog was tied up on a 10-metre lead but managed to walk 200 metres. How was this possible?

Q20. How do you divide five apples between five children in such a way that ensures each child gets an apple and an apple remains in the basket?

Round 5
Countries and cities that no longer exist
Let's find out how well you know countries and capitals that no longer exist or exist under a different name. Oh, and read the question!

Q21. Here is my picture of a British cathedral with the tallest spire in the country. The city where it stands was the old name of a capital city. What is that capital city now called?

Q22. Name this former country.

Q23. Take a look at this image, which contains two capital cities, one former and one current. Name the country.

Q24. This country no longer exists. What was it called?

Q25. Here is a formula I have made from flags. The third flag is made of the flags of two former countries. What country has the third flag?

Round 6
Connections

Q26. Audrey Hepburn's what sold at auction in 2006 for £467,000?

Q27. In this adaptation, a beautiful princess is locked away by the evil Mother Gothel but rescued by the handsome Flynn Rider. The princess is well-known for her incredibly long what?

Q28. What name is shared by Pendleton and Derbyshire?

Q29. What can be blanket, back, whip and running?

Q30. The Chinook helicopter, VW Scirocco and the Mistral missile are all named after what?

Q31. What famous race begins in France and ends in Senegal on the West coast of Africa? I am most interested in the type of race.

Q32. So, what's the connection?

113

QUIZ No. 30

Round 1
Cryptic film titles

I have disguised the titles of well-known films for you here. For example, if I said 'Rutland Water Mutts', you'd instantly know I was talking about that Tarantino classic *Reservoir Dogs*.

Q1. Armed Bloke Chasing Elk

Q2. Grubby Bopping

Q3. Starting Where I'm Sitting and Ending at Infinitude

Q4. A Land Where Only Young Males Can Live

Q5. Certainly Not The First Flexer of Nitrogen and Oxygen

Round 2
NFL

This is a good example of a niche round. Not everyone knows much about the National Football League, so these questions are designed to level the playing field.

Q6. The following are all sports teams from New York. Which one is an American Football team?

YANKEES – KNICKS – GIANTS – RANGERS

Q7. The owners of the Tampa Bay Buccaneers also own a Premier League football team. Which one?

Q8. ANGRY ABC KEEPERS is an anagram of which NFL team, the winner of the very first Super Bowl in 1967?

Q9. What famous actor and convicted kidnapper, armed robber and murderer played for the Buffalo Bills and the San Francisco 49ers?

Q10. In 2020, the half time show at the Superbowl had two headline acts performing together. One was Shakira. Who was the other?

Round 3
Lead singers
Name both the groups pictured and the lead singer I have obscured.

Q11.   Q12.

Q13.   Q14.

Q15.

Round 4
Italy
Q16. What is the capital of Sicily?
Q17. The famous Italian football team Juventus are from which Italian city?

Q18. The Teenage Mutant Ninja Turtles are named after four famous Italian artists. Raphael, Michelangelo and Leonardo are three. Who is the fourth?

Q19. One product, in its true form, is made from pressed Trebbiano and Lambrusco grapes and aged for a minimum of 12 years in several barrels of successively smaller sizes, each made of a different wood. When bottled with a white-coloured cap, you know the product has been aged for 12 years; with a silver cap – at least 18 years; with a gold cap – 25 years and more. What is the name of this product?

Q20. A famous horse race is held in an ancient Italian city. It appears in the James Bond film *A Quantum of Solace*. What's the city?

Round 5
Missing landmarks
I show you pictures of famous landmarks, only without the landmarks. You tell me what is missing.

Q21. Q22.

Q23. Q24.

Q25.

Round 6
Connections

Q26. The monument to Charles the First in London marks Mile Zero in the capital, from where all distances to and from London are measured. This monument stands in front of a famous square. What is that square called?

Q27. What connects Bella the vampire lover, Graham the cricketer and a famous brand of matches?

Q28. According to legend, the White Tower would fall if what left the Tower of London?

Q29. What rare and prestigious children's TV programme award is held, among others, by Sir David Attenborough, Tim Peake, the late Captain Sir Tom Moore, Marcus Rashford and Greta Thunberg?

Q30. What famous road junction in central London was used as a codeword to announce to the government the death of George VI?

Q31. When discovered in rough form, this item weighed 621g. It was since broken into nine individual pieces, each priceless. The nine items are named after the the chairman of the place where it was discovered, with '_____ I' being the largest in the world and '_____ II', the second. What was the surname of the chairman?

Q32. So, what's the connection?

QUIZ No. 31

Round 1
In the news
(6 June 2022)

Q1. This week, West Ham footballer Kurt Zouma was given 180 hours of community service for kicking what?

Q2. Former *Great British Bake Off* winner Frances Quinn baked the world's largest what this week? It weighs 80kg and has a diameter of 175 cm.

Q3. To mark the Queen's Jubilee, Heinz has renamed two of its household brands. Name one of the new brands for the point.

Q4. Why has the logo for the Wincanton Town Festival in Dorset, designed to mark the Jubilee, caused a bit of a stir online?

Q5. Still and sparkling wines from which English county have joined Welsh lamb, Melton Mowbray pork pies and Cornish clotted cream to have been awarded geographically protected status?

Round 2
Platinum Jubilee
Questions about the life of the Queen.

Q6. What did the Queen call the year 1992, when there was a fire at Windsor Castle, explosive revelations emerged from books about Princess Diana, and the Duchess of York was revealed to have had an affair with her financial advisor?

Q7. In 1977, the Sex Pistols' single *God Save The Queen* reached No.2 in the official UK singles chart despite being banned from radio play by the BBC. It was pipped to the top spot by the song *I Don't Want to Talk About It*, but who sang that song?

Q8. Who was the Queen's father?

Q9. In what city was the Queen born?

Q10. The Queen has official residences in each of the countries of the United Kingdom. What is the Queen's official residence in Northern Ireland called?

Round 3
Sydmar Lodge album covers
Residents of the Sydmar Lodge care home recreated famous album covers. Your job: give me the name of the original album and artist for each album cover you see.

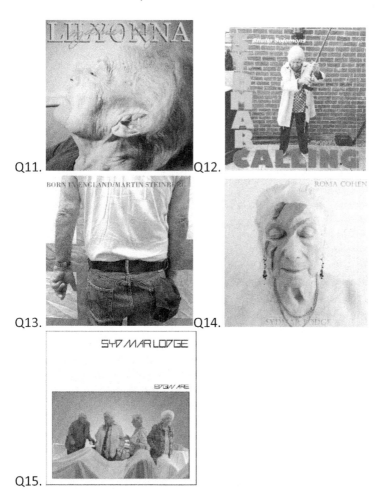

Q11.

Q12.

Q13.

Q14.

Q15.

Round 4
Songs with boy's names in the title

Q16. In his famous song, Paul Simon says you can call him what?

Q17. Janis Joplin sang a song called *Me and _____ who*?

Q18. Gorillaz had a famous song about a famous actor and director. The anagram of his first and last names is WIDEST COOLANT.

Q19. Coldplay have a famous single named after a famous cartoon character. What's it called?

Q20. Here are some lyrics to a famous song that is a one-word boy's name. Name it.

'You were fifteen
I was twelve
It was summer
We were so in love
I never loved anyone this much
Look at me
I'm thrilled to your touch
Hey ____, do you remember me?
____, do you remember me?'

Round 5
Famous maps and journeys

Q21. Of what is this a map?   Q22. Of what is this map?

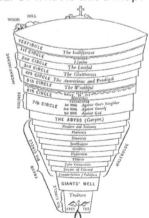   

Q23. Of what is this a map?

Q24. What was the name of the story about Bodger, Tao and Luath, who cross the Canadian wilderness in search of the Hunter family?

Q25. This map was drawn by a famous writer, but can you name the book it accompanies?

Round 6

Connections

Q26. Which artist had the first names Joseph Mallord William?

Q27. The villain in Ian Fleming's *Live and Let Die*, Dr Kananga, has an alter-ego drug baron. What is that alter-ego's name?

Q28. What is the largest city in Pennsylvania and the home of a museum of art, the steps up to which were immortalised in Sylvester Stallone's triumphant run in the film *Rocky*?

Q29. What 15-16th century Italian is attributed with inventing the parachute and the calculator and with harnessing solar power?

Q30. What is the name of Princess Anne's first husband?

Q31. What publication closed in July 2011 with the headline THANK YOU AND GOODBYE?

Q32. So, what's the connection?

QUIZ No. 32

Round 1
Summer
A music round where all the titles contain the word SUMMER.

Q1. Who is *Looking for the Summer* in his famous song?

Q2. Name the artist who performs the song with the following lyric:
    'If her daddy's rich, take her out for a meal
    If her daddy's poor, just do what you feel.'

Q3. Don Henley had a solo hit called *Boys of Summer*. He was the founding member of which famous rock band?

Q4. Bananarama had a top 10 hit in the 80s that contains the word SUMMER. What is it called?

Q5. Lana Del Ray sings about *Summertime WHAT?*

Round 2
Religious festivals
Q6. What is the name of the holy day where the Pope traditionally washes and kisses the feet of twelve people, and the Queen gives coins to deserving senior citizens?

Q7. In popular belief, if it rains on what religious festival it will rain for another 40 days?

Q8. FOOTMEN EAT ANDY is an anagram of what religious festival?

Q9. What religious festival day comes after the day when we traditionally eat pancakes?

Q10. This Hindu festival translates as 'Rows of Lighted Lamps'. What is it called?

Round 3
Golf
If you like golf, these next five should suit you to a tee. If you don't, you'll have to bunker down and hope your discussions don't drive a wedge between you.

Q11. Golfers compete for this trophy in what competition?

Q12. This is the logo for which golf tournament?

Q13. This is the location of which famous golf course?

Q14. This is the clubhouse at which famous golf course?

Q15. For the final question in the round, based on the theme of the round, name the woman on the left

Round 4
Oscar winners

Q16. The poster for an Oscar-winning film features an image of a car's rear-view mirror reflecting a chauffeur in a hat at the wheel and a woman, also wearing a hat, on the back seat. What is the film called?

Q17. What is the name of the film that won the first-ever Oscar for a female best director?

Q18. Sean Connery was famous for his role in seven James Bond films. But for which film did he receive his only Oscar?

Q19. In 1986, a story about Karen Blixen won numerous Oscars. Karen, abandoned by her husband, ends up in the arms of Denys Finch Hatton, a British adventurer and pilot. What is the film called?

Q20. 'What's the most you ever lost on a coin toss?' is a quote from which Oscar-winning film?

Round 5
Merged faces
Name both people in each picture. Each pair share a profession.

Q21.   Q22.

Q23.   Q24.   Q25.

Round 6
Connections

Q26. Who wrote the book *Under Milk Wood*?

Q27. What is the famous catchphrase in the sitcom called *Diff'rent Strokes*?

Q28. What type of queue is also a brand name synonymous with bananas and pineapples?

Q29. What was the name of the first ghost to visit Ebeneezer Scrooge?

Q30. What do Burma, Siberia and Cornwall all have in common?

Q31. Napoleon Solo and Ilya Kuryakin are the main characters in what 1960s action drama?

Q32. So, what's the connection?

QUIZ No. 33

Round 1
In the news
(20 June 2022)

Q1. A recent BBC crime drama, currently on iPlayer, is set in Nottinghamshire and bears the name of a district of Nottingham. What is it called?

Q2. Complete this headline from an edition of Metro newspaper last week: *Keir says Boris 'thinks he's Obi-Wan Kenobi, when he's really _____ '*

Q3. Andrew Redmayne is the substitute goalkeeper who danced on the line before saving the deciding penalty to send his country to this year's World Cup. What country does he represent?

Q4. What spin-off film from the *Toy Story* franchise has received mixed reviews since its recent release at the box office?

Q5. In order to keep the country's economy afloat, People in Pakistan have been asked to reduce their consumption of what? Pakistan is the world's largest importer of this product.

Round 2
Famous people in anagram form

Q6. THAT GREAT CHARMER is an anagram of what famous politician?

Q7. ASHIEST MINER is an anagram of what famous artist?

Q8. GENUINE CLASS is an anagram of what famous actor?

Q9. NICE SILKY WOMAN is an anagram of what famous intern?

Q10. WEIRDOS KNOW ALBERT is the name of what famous footballer?

Round 3
The Robert picture round

Q11. Name this famous Robert from the world of music

Q12. Here's a dashing actor called Robert. What's his surname?

Q13. This is a famous Scottish writer whose most famous works were published in the 1880s. Who is he?

Q14. This American is famous for saying, 'Now I am become death, the destroyer of worlds'. Who was he?

Q15. This Robert is a film director. His first movie was made on a budget of $7000, funded by his putting himself through medical research. The film was remade with production by Quentin Tarantino and renamed *Desperado*, starring Antonio Banderas.

Round 4
Cover versions of songs
Q16. Whitney Houston is famous for her number-one song *I Will Always Love You*, which featured in the film *The Bodyguard*. Who wrote and performed the original of this song?
Q17. UB40 are famous for the song *Red Red Wine*, but it wasn't UB40 who wrote and first performed it. Who did?
Q18. The (English) Beat had a song called *Can't Get Used To Losing You*. What old crooner wrote and originally performed it?
Q19. A famous number one single features the performer shedding a real tear during the recording of the video. The original was written and performed by Prince, but what is the song called?
Q20. The inimitable Screamin Jay Hawkins wrote the original of this song. It has been covered by Nina Simone, Annie Lennox, Bryan Ferry, Sonique, Joe Cocker and Creedence Clearwater Revival, to name but a few. What is the song called?

Round 5
Animal kingdom
Q21. What creature lives in these?

Q22. What is this?

Q23. What is this creature?

Q24. With its distinctive colouring, what type of fish is this?

Q25. And what is the name of this butterfly?

Round 6
Connections

Q26. Who was the last Queen of France before the French Revolution?

Q27. Which world leader allegedly banged his shoe on the podium at the UN General Assembly in 1960?

Q28. An actor called George, an American politician called John, a singer-songwriter called Brian, and a Liverpool footballer called Alan all shared the same surname. What was it?

Q29. The French equivalent of the *umlaut* is the tréma. It is used in names such as 'Citroën' and means the two vowels are pronounced separately. What brand of champagne contains a tréma?

Q30. The world's most expensive food is called Almas and comes from Iran. A kilo of this stuff will cost you about $34,500. What is it?

Q31. In the United Kingdom, what contains 22 seats, of which only six are currently occupied by women?

Q32. So, what's the connection?

QUIZ No. 34

Round 1
Things that don't come from where we think they do
Q1. What is the name of the hat that actually comes from Ecuador, although it bears the name of a different country?

Q2. French fries don't actually come from France. Where do they come from?

Q3. The French horn and the English horn are not actually from France or England. In what country did they originate?

Q4. Guess what? Danish pastries aren't from Denmark. In what country did they actually originate?

Q5. The Molotov Cocktail, a bottle containing petrol and a burning rag, is not a Soviet or Russian invention but that of a country that was embroiled in the so-called Winter War with the Soviet Union in November 1939. Name that country.

Round 2
Who am I?
I give you clues; you tell me about whom I am talking.

Q6. My parents' names were Frances and John. My brother and husband were both called Charles. I had two sons; one now lives in London and one in the USA. Who am I?

Q7. I was born in Zanzibar to Parsi-Indian parents. My singing range covers four octaves. Who am I?

Q8. I was King of England but never married. My complexion and hair colour gave me the nickname by which I am best known. I died in suspicious circumstances when I was shot while out hunting. Who am I?

Q9. I was born in Skegness. I began my football playing career with Scunthorpe United before moving to Liverpool, where I played for most of my career. I died in November 2020. Who am I?

Q10. I was born in 1935. I like pickled cucumbers, I erected the world's largest tent, and my river crossing is rather wobbly. Who am I?

Round 3
Really bad statues
Can you name these famous people from their bad statues?

Q11.

Q12.

Q13.

Q14.

Q15.

Round 4

Fashion

Q16. An easy one to start with. What fashion item did Elvis ask you not to step on?

Q17. What first lady had a shoe collection of more than 3,000 pairs, which now make up a museum to illustrate the opulent lifestyle of that country's leaders?

Q18. What do the fashion houses of Hermes, Longchamp and Ralph Lauren all have in common?

Q19. The Four-in-hand, Oriental, Kelvin, Grantchester, Eldredge and Café are all types of what, something traditionally associated with men's fashion?

Q20. What fashion designer designed the kit for the British Olympic team in 2012 and 2016?

Round 5

Film mash-ups

Name the two films pictured in these mash-ups I have created.

 Q21.  Q22.

 Q23.  Q24.

Q25.

Round 6
Connections

Q26. Lyric time. Who performs the song with the following lyrics:
'Walked out this morning, I don't believe what I saw
Hundred billion bottles washed up on the shore
Seems I'm not alone at being alone
Hundred billion castaways, looking for a home.'?

Q27. What group performed the song *The Hooded Man* that accompanied the TV drama *Robin of Sherwood* in the mid-1980s?

Q28. What group had hit songs called *The Invisible Man*, *Kayleigh* and *Lavender*?

Q29. In 2008, what group sang:
'I'm so three thousand and eight
You so two thousand and late'?
We'll forgive them for the abysmal grammar, I suppose.

Q30. A word clue for the next one:
Say my name, soldier with brown eyes; I'm dangerously in love and lose my breath with emotion.
Six songs by what group make up this frankly daft sentence?

Q31. When ITV won the rights to broadcast the Premiership from 2001 to 2004, who performed the theme tune?

Q32. So, what's the connection?

QUIZ No. 35

Round 1
Cockney Rhyming Slang for parts of the body
You know how this works: TROUBLE is short for TROUBLE AND STRIFE, which means WIFE. The following answers, however, are all parts of the body.
Q1. If you say your plates are killing you, what is hurting?
Q2. If someone says you have lovely minces, to what are they referring?
Q3. If I've had my Jimi taken out, what does my body no longer possess?
Q4. If someone wants a Dicky in your Bottle, to which body part of yours are they referring?
Q5. For the last one, I want you to translate the following: I'VE GOT NO HAMPSTEADS IN MY NORTH.

Round 2
Famous lines and catchphrases
Q6. The line 'You're gonna need a bigger boat' comes from what film?
Q7. The quote 'You ain't heard nothin' yet!' comes from what famous film?
Q8. These are lyrics from what famous song?
     'No, I can't bear to live my life alone
     I grow impatient for a love to call my own
     But when I feel that I, I can't go on
     Well these precious words keep me hanging on.'
Q9. What famous cartoon character's catchphrase is 'That's all I can stands, I can't stands no more'?
Q10. What cartoon character has the catchphrase 'Sufferin Succotash!'?

Round 3
Bits of famous paintings
These are bits of famous paintings. Can you name them?

Q11.   Q12.

Q13.   Q14.

Q15. This last one is part of an illustration from *The Final Problem*. Where is this illustration set?

Round 4
Sports equipment

Q16. What sport uses finger tabs, chest guards and quivers?

Q17. A workshop in Ayrshire uses granite from the island of Ailsa Craig to make particular items weighing 20kg. These items are the only ones used in competition by the World Federation of this sport. What sport?

Q18. What sport is played on a mat measuring six feet by three feet, using squidgers measuring from 1 to 2 inches in diameter and a pot of about 2 inches in diameter?

Q19. In what pursuit would you use cordelette, a bag of chalk and a belay device?

Q20. What sport uses a 17-foot-long piece of a fir tree?

Round 5
Picture clues for songs and films

Q21. Can you name the song title from this picture code?

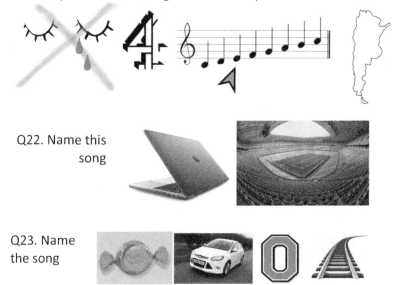

Q22. Name this song

Q23. Name the song

Q24. Which REM song is depicted here?

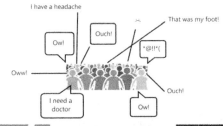

Q25. Name the film

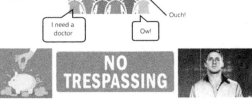

Round 6
Connections

Q26. Who was the leader of the Liberal Democrats from 2017 to 2019?

Q27. What transport job was phased out across the country in the 1980s and finally abolished altogether in London in 2005?

Q28. What is the third planet from the sun, a distance of about 93 million miles?

Q29. What type of footwear actually means a sudden or unexpected reversal, as in direction, belief or attitude?

Q30. What do Willesden, Clapham, Dalston and Watford railway stations all have in common?

Q31. Brian Johnson replaced Bon Scott in 1980 as the lead singer of what group?

Q32. So, what's the connection?

QUIZ No. 36

Round 1
Superstitions
Q1. This item is considered to be a good luck charm in a wide range of cultures. Belief in its magical powers traces back to the Greeks, who thought the element iron could ward off evil. Shaped like a crescent moon, this item was also a symbol of fertility and good fortune. What is it?
Q2. The ancient Egyptians placed an item in tombs to assist the dead in their journey to heaven. They believed that the space between the tomb wall and this item, which leaned against it, harboured good and evil spirits which should not be disturbed. What is this item?
Q3. According to the old British superstition, what will fall if the ravens leave the Tower of London?
Q4. What should you throw some of over your left shoulder to ward off evil spirits?
Q5. Judas at the Last Supper and Loki, who crashed the feast of gods in Valhalla, have what number in common?

Round 2
Phrases or sayings as they appear in other languages
Q6. The Germans say, 'The morning hour has gold in its mouth'. What do we say?
Q7. In Mandarin Chinese, when someone tells a story that is long-winded and contains unnecessary information, they are said to be drawing feet on a what?
Q8. The Spanish phrase 'To grab someone's hair' is the equivalent of what English saying?
Q9. The Italians use the phrase 'With every death of a pope'. What do we say?
Q10. In Russian, a bad male ballet dancer says his balls get in the way. What is the equivalent phrase in English?

Round 3
Avatars
Name these famous people from their avatars.

Q11.   Q12.   Q13.

Q14.   Q15.

Round 4
Science and technology
Q16. Who is the first person and the only woman to win a Nobel prize twice, in two scientific fields?

Q17. RELAX, ALHAMBRA LEGEND is an anagram of what famous inventor?

Q18. The European Particle Physics Laboratory is better known by what abbreviation?

Q19. Who ran naked through Syracuse after discovering the buoyancy principle?

Q20. ERNIE TREMBLES is another anagram of a famous scientist and inventor. Who?

Round 5
Close-ups photos
These images are close-ups of things you can find around the home

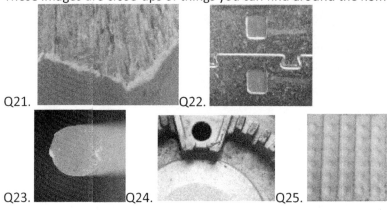

Q21.　　　　　　　　　Q22.

Q23.　　　　Q24.　　　　　　Q25.

Round 6
Connections
Q26. What do the lead singer of Dire Straits, the head of Facebook and the actor who has played the Incredible Hulk most in Marvel movies have in common?
Q27. David Tennant, Tony Curtis and Heath Ledger have all played what sexy character in the movies?
Q28. The Duke of Wellington had a horse with the name of a capital city. What capital city is that?
Q29. Who wrote the British TV series *The Office* alongside Ricky Gervais? In 2021, he starred in, co-wrote, co-produced, and co-directed the 12-part comedy crime series *The Outlaws*.
Q30. What is the longest human-made waterway in the United Kingdom?
Q31. Who wrote the hold music that, in 2020, the Department for Work and Pensions replaced on its telephone helplines, as many found its repetitiveness disturbing?
Q32. So, what's the connection?

QUIZ No. 37

Round 1
Sporting disqualifications

Q1. Arguably, the most famous Olympic cheat was Ben Johnson, the fastest man alive in 1988, who had his gold medal taken from him for being off his head on drugs. What was his nationality?

Q2. British athlete Chijindu Ujah was found guilty of a doping offence at the 2020 Olympics. This offence led to him being stripped of his medal in which event?

Q3. Why was the 1904 Olympic marathon champion Fred Lorz disqualified?

Q4. What is the name of the British football referee who showed Croatian Josip Simunic three yellow cards during the 2006 World Cup before eventually doing the maths and sending the offender from the field?

Q5. The rivalry between Kerrigan and Harding in the 1990s became the subject of a famous film. What was the sport?

Round 2
Famous and infamous women

Q6. Who broke the women's altitude record in 1922 when she rose to 14,000 feet?

Q7. What did Rosa Parks refuse to do in 1955?

Q8. What was Ada Lovelace's main field of activity? A famous institute now bears her name.

Q9. According to the American Film Institute's '100 Years...100 Stars' listing of the top 25 male and 25 female greatest screen legends, who tops the list of women?

Q10. From what did Peg Entwistle jump to her death in 1932 after failing to achieve her dreams of stardom?

Round 3
Badly drawn celebrities

Yep, these are pretty rubbish but strangely recognisable at the same time. Do YOU recognise them?

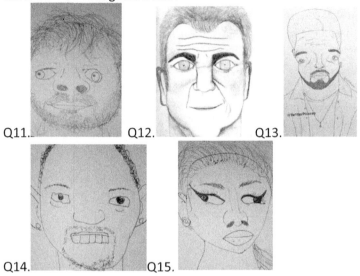

Q11.

Q12.

Q13.

Q14.

Q15.

Round 4
Arithmetic, sort of

Q16. Multiply the number of Heinz varieties by Cristiano Ronaldo's shirt number at Manchester United

Q17. Add the number that follows BLINK in the rock band name to the number that follows SHAM in the punk band name

Q18. If a golfer plays a full eighteen holes and posts a highly unlikely five pars, two bogeys, three double-bogeys, three birdies, three eagles, one albatross and one condor, what is their score as they leave the 18th green?

Q19. Add the highest possible out shot (or finish) in darts to the value of the pink ball in snooker

Q20. This one is not really arithmetic... or is it?

8 + 8 = 4. How is this possible?

Round 5
Famous doors

Q21. This is the door to what famous building?

Q22. To what does this door lead (I have blocked out the answer)?

Q23. Here is an annotated drawing of a famous door. On what building would you find it?

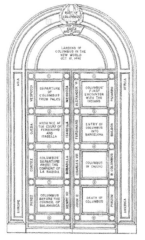

Q24. This is the front door from what TV show?

Q25. Here is an iconic image from a film. What line is spoken after this chap presses his button?

Round 6

Connections

Q26. This famous rocker has only been married once, although many believe he was actually married to the woman who is now getting divorced from Rupert Murdoch. Name the famous rocker.

Q27. Sheriff Pat Garrett famously shot who?

Q28. Who has been a taxi driver, a king of comedy, an intern and a dirty grandpa?

Q29. Who is considered to have started the trend of wearing a white wedding dress? Clue: she proposed to her husband, most unusual for the time.

Q30. What famous Russian is alleged to have said, 'Despite my terrible sins, I am a Christ in miniature'?

Q31. According to a recent survey, 12% of Americans believe that who was the wife of Noah?

Q32. So, what's the connection?

QUIZ No. 38

Round 1
Detective sidekicks and helpers
Q1. Mrs Hudson cleans whose apartment?
Q2. Captain Arthur Hastings is which detective's frequent companion?
Q3. Maddy Magellan is the original sidekick of which famous TV detective?
Q4. Danny Williams is whose sidekick?
Q5. Richard Poole and Camille Bordey were the original crime-fighting team in what TV series?

Round 2
Things that happened on 8th August
Q6. Name the famous Swiss sportsperson who was born on 8th August 1981
Q7. Name the famous criminal event that took place on 8th August 1963
Q8. Name the President who famously resigned on 8th August 1974
Q9. What is the name of the famous bell tower, the construction of which began on 8th August 1173
Q10. On 8th August 1992, the US men's Olympic basketball team, dubbed 'The Dream Team', easily won gold with players including Michael Jordan and Magic Johnson. But who did they beat to win gold?

Round 3
Famous Ukrainians
Use your U-kranium to work these out.

Q11.   Q12.   Q13.

Q14.   Q15.

Round 4
Board games
Q16. How many individual squares are there on a chess board?
Q17. The classic version of what game of skill and strategy uses 136 tiles?
Q18. What is the only letter in Scrabble to score 5 points?
Q19. What is the most expensive orange property in Monopoly?
Q20. The board game Cluedo has ten rooms, including the cellar. However, it used to have eleven. Which room was removed?

Round 5
Emojis for food and drinks brands

Q21. Name this famous drinks brand.

Q22. Name this famous food brand.

Q23. Name this fast food chain.

Q24. Name this food brand.

Q25. Name this brand of snack food.

Round 6
Connections

I need a specific answer for the connection.

Q26. Name the actor who won her first Oscar for her role in *The Favourite*.

Q27. What will Olympians be able to do on the South Pacific island of Tahiti for the 2024 Paris Olympics?

Q28. What comes next in this sequence:

18, 15, 12, 12A ___?

Q29. What branded beverage do you get when you take bourbon whiskey, add vanilla bean, lemon, cinnamon, cloves, cherries, a bit of orange and then some honey?

Q30. With what fruit would you associate the Friends actor Matthew, the pop singer Katy and the tennis player Fred?

Q31. According to the nursery rhyme, who went fishing for a whale in a bucket of water?

Q32. So, what's the connection?

QUIZ No. 39

Round 1
Opening lines from famous songs
Just name the song.
Q1. I've never seen you looking so lovely as you did tonight
Q2. Every now and then I get a little bit lonely
Q3. I light a candle to our love
Q4. I walked in the cold air
Q5. When I was a boy, just about the 8th Grade

Round 2
Guess the food based on the recipe ingredients
Q6. What dish do you get when you use spaghetti, eggs, parmesan, pancetta and garlic?
Q7. What dish do you get when you use lime juice, salt, onion, jalapeno pepper and avocado?
Q8. What sauce do you get when you use olive oil, vinegar, garlic, oregano, red chilli flakes and parsley?
Q9. What do you get when you put lemon zest, juice, sugar and butter in a heatproof bowl over a pan of simmering water, stir and then whisk in a beaten egg and stir again until thickened?
Q10. What dish do you get when you stir-fry rice noodles, shrimp, chicken, or tofu, peanuts, scrambled egg and bean sprouts with fish sauce, oyster sauce, brown sugar and tamarind?

Round 3
Picture connections
Q11. Here are three pictures from films. What connects them?

Q12. What connects these three?

Q13. Here are four famous faces. Name the composer who comes next in the list

Q14. What one word connects the following:

 119 seconds THE MAN IN THE WHITE SUIT

Q15. What work of literature connects these three?

Round 4
The commonest and most popular
Q16. What animal is the most popular pet in the UK?

Q17. As of today, what is the commonest species of tree in the British Isles?

Q18. What was the most popular model of car in the UK in 2021, although it is now being discontinued?

Q19. What is Britain's most popular football club in terms of Instagram, Facebook, Twitter and YouTube subscribers?

Q20. What is the commonest coin in circulation in the UK?

Round 5
Album covers
How many of these albums can you name?

Q21.   Q22.   Q23.

Q24.   Q25.

Round 6
Connections
Q26. What is the surname of the actor Miranda, who was nominated for an Oscar for her role in *Tom and Viv* and who has also starred in *The Hours*, *Spider* and *Made in Dagenham*?

Q27. What is the surname of English actor and comedian Steve, who is best known as a member of *The League of Gentlemen* along with Mark Gatiss?

Q28. What famous darts player has the nickname *The King of Bling*?

Q29. What is the missing word in the famous Charlie Chaplin film *A _____ in New York*?

Q30. What is the surname of Karen, a former England women's footballer and now a broadcaster on Sky Sports?

Q31. What is the proper name for the inner courtyard in the middle of a castle?

Q32. So, what's the connection?

QUIZ No. 40

Round 1
I'll have a P, please Bob

One of my favourite quiz shows in the 1980s was *Blockbusters*, which famously included the line 'I'll have a P, please, Bob'. In honour of that favourite of mine, this round features a total mixed bag of questions where the answers all begin with the letter P.

Q1. What is the name of the Disney character who can fly and who never grows up?

Q2. NEVER ODD OR EVEN is an example of what?

Q3. The title of one of Beatrix Potter's stories has three words in the title that begin with the letter P. What is that story? (it actually contains more than three words, but three of the total number begin with a P)

Q4. Who performs the song with the following lyrics:

'O.K.
Just a little pin prick
There'll be no more aaaaaaaah!
But you may feel a little sick'

Q5. This last one doesn't actually start with P but is about the letter P. Take the names and surnames of the four Goons and tell me how many Ps they contain in total.

Round 2
Friends

Q6. What colour is the settee in the opening sequence of *Friends*?

Q7. Between working as a waitress in the coffee house and as a buyer at Ralph Lauren, in what department store does Rachel work in *Friends*?

Q8. Anagram time. GOALPOST ELATION is an anagram of the profession of one of the *Friends* characters. Name that profession.

Q9. The name of which *Friends* character is the same as the name of a person who makes candles?

151

Q10. A proper *Friends* question to end the round. What is the name of Phoebe's twin sister in *Friends*?

Round 3
Disney characters
Name these five Disney characters.

Q11.   Q12.   Q13.

Q14.   Q15.

Round 4
Alloys
Q16. Brass is an alloy of copper and what other predominant metal? It may also contain small amounts of lead, silicon, tin, iron, aluminium and manganese, but the second metal is always found in greater quantities.

Q17. What is the principal metal in pewter, accounting for a minimum of 85%?

Q18. Steel is an alloy made of iron and carbon. What element is added to make it stainless steel?

Q19. What is the name of the alloy used principally in dentistry, which is produced by mixing liquid mercury with an alloy made of silver, tin, and solid copper particles?

Q20. GRIM RIB BATH is an anagram of a lightweight sheet metal used predominantly in car bodies, mostly old Land Rovers.

Round 5
Fused animals
Name the creatures that make up each of these odd creations.

Q21.   Q22.   Q23.

Q24.   Q25.

Round 6
Connections
Q26. The film *The Theory of Everything*, about the life of Stephen Hawking, is set predominantly in what city?
Q27. To mark the Queen's Platinum Jubilee, eight UK towns were given city status. Only one is in Yorkshire. What is it called?
Q28. What city is home to the Rijksmuseum?
Q29. The silhouette of what famous sports star was used by Nike for its Jumpman logo on a range of trainers?
Q30. In what city did Alan Wells win gold in the 100m, although we have since learned he was off his head on drugs at the time?
Q31. The flag of what country features a wheel in its centre?
Q32. So, what's the connection?

QUIZ No. 41

Round 1
Music and film
I will give you a couple of clues, one of which is musical. You give me the answer, which is either a film or something about a film.

Q1. What is Demi Moore holding when the Righteous Brothers sing *Unchained Melody*?

Q2. In what famous film are Sonny and Cher singing *I Got You Babe* when the alarm clock changes to 6 a.m.?

Q3. What does Robin Williams scream into a microphone in the film that features Louis Armstrong singing *It's a Wonderful World*?

Q4. What film contains the line 'Forget everything else and just say it to me. Say it to me as a friend'? After this line, the central character speaks, with the Second Movement of Beethoven's *Symphony No. 7* playing in the background.

Q5. In what film does Piers Brosnan say 'Let's play ball' before he dons a bowler hat to the Nina Simone classic *Sinnerman*?

Round 2
Peaky Blinders
Q6. Who wrote the original theme song to *Peaky Blinders*? It's called *Red Right Hand*.

Q7. What is the name of the pub that is the central focus for the Shelby clan?

Q8. The creator of *Peaky Blinders* co-created what hugely popular television quiz show?

Q9. Helen McCrory trained to master the Birmingham dialect by watching endless clips of what famous lead singer?

Q10. The actors Tom Hardy and Charlotte Riley, who both appear in *Peaky Blinders*, are married. They met while filming in 2009 as the central characters in what famous period drama for ITV?

Round 3
Song titles in picture clue form

Q11.   Q12.

Q13.   Q14.

Q15.

Round 4
Famous moves in sport
Q16. The so-called Fosbury Flop revolutionised which Olympic sport?
Q17. What do you call the penalty technique in football that fools the goalie with a gentle chip into the middle of the goal?
Q18. This was a move first used in the 1974 World Cup. The player shaped as if to pass the ball but then dragged the ball behind his standing leg with the inside of his foot. He then turned his body 180 degrees and raced off, making the opponent look a bit of a Muppet. Who first performed this move, giving his name to the manoeuvre?
Q19. The Blank, the Blank 2, the Blank on the Floor and the Blank on the Vault are all signature moves by a single sportsperson, whose

name I have replaced with BLANK. What is the actual surname I have replaced?

Q20. The 360 bar spin, the suicide no-hander, the foot plant and the can-can are all moves in which Olympic sport?

Round 5
What is wrong?
Say what is wrong with the following pictures

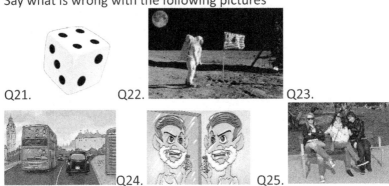

Q21.　　　　　　Q22.　　　　　　　　　Q23.

Q24.　　　　　　Q25.

Round 6
Connections
Q26. What is the longest human-made structure in the world?

Q27. What actor has played Nelson Mandela, God and a prisoner called Red?

Q28. Francis Drake was mayor of what city in 1581?

Q29. The current four judges on *Britain's Got Talent* are Simon Cowell, Alesha Dixon, David Walliams and who else?

Q30. What is a subatomic particle with a positive electrical charge that is found in the nucleus of every atom?

Q31. Phil replaced Peter in 1975 as the lead singer of what group?

Q32. So, what's the connection?

QUIZ No. 42

Round 1
Fruit and veg
I give you three varieties; you tell me of what.
Q1. FUJI, EMPIRE, BRAEBURN
Q2. GRAPE, HEIRLOOM, BEEFSTEAK
Q3. CHANTENAY, ADELAIDE, DANVERS
Q4. ALBION, ALPINE ALEXANDRIA, WENDY
Q5. TIMPERLEY EARLY, HARDY TARTY, PRINCE ALBERT

Round 2
Dimensions
Q6. Which standard British coin, currently in circulation, has a diameter of 24.5mm?
Q7. Which size of paper measures 420mm x 594mm?
Q8. What historical document is about 71 metres long but only 51 centimetres high?
Q9. What item of sports equipment measures 45.7 cm across and stands 3 metres off the ground?
Q10. What structure in Britain, completed in 128 AD, is 73 miles long, coast to coast?

Round 3
Combined logos
Name the two brands that appear in each image

Q11.   Q12.   Q13.

Q14.   Q15.

Round 4
Cryptic clues for music bands and groups
Q16. BA-BSC-MBA
Q17. Not death in the Orient
Q18. Too many occupants living here
Q19. Monarchs of Seat saloon car
Q20. George, David, Andrew, Patrick

Round 5
A Question of Sport – What Happened Next

Q21. Here is a famous picture from the football World Cup. What happened next?

Q22. This is Lazaro Borges, a pole-vaulter from Cuba competing at the 2012 Olympic Games in London. What happened next?

Q23. We all recognise Usain Bolt, of course, and here he is after just winning Gold for the 200m in the 2015 World Championships. What happened after this photo was taken?

 Q24. This is boxer Tyson Fury with his man on the ropes. Things, however, didn't go quite to plan for Fury, and the result is a famous gif. What happened next?

Q25. 2015 A doubles semi-final at Wimbledon, with Jamie Murry about to serve an ace. The ball bounced high and was caught by someone famous in the royal box. By whom?

Round 6
Connections
Q26. In addition to their famous song *Money, Money, Money*, ABBA had another number-one single that featured one word, repeated three times in succession. What is it called?

Q27. Marcus Mumford, lead singer of Mumford and Sons, is married to the star of *The Great Gatsby*, *An Education* and *Drive*. What is her name?

Q28. What age in history began in approximately 1200 BC and is thought by most scholars to have ended in around 55 BC?

Q29. In the popular TV game show, what would team captains Lee Mack and David Mitchell supposedly not do to each other?

Q30. Robin Williams played the hero and Dustin Hoffman, the eponymous villain, in what film?

Q31. What colour is also the surname of the villain in James Bond's *A Quantum of Solace*?

Q32. So, what's the connection?

QUIZ No. 43

Round 1
Queen Elizabeth II
Q1. In what year did the Queen make her first Christmas broadcast?
Q2. The Queen had a number of hobbies, including horse riding, pigeon racing and even football. But what football team did she support?
Q3. The Queen's first what was called Peggy?
Q4. When the Queen married, she purchased the material for her wedding dress herself, returning the many donations from women around the UK. But what did she use to pay for the material?
Q5. What was the date of the Queen's actual birthday?

Round 2
Voiceovers
Q6. Who made the voice of Darth Vader his own in the *Star Wars* films?
Q7. Whose original narration for the live radio version of *The War of the Worlds* incited panic by making some members of the listening audience believe that a Martian invasion was actually taking place?
Q8. Who famously voiced these lyrics at the end of a number-one single?

> 'Darkness falls across the land
> The midnight hour is close at hand
> Creatures call in search of blood
> To terrorise your neighbourhood.'

Q9. The makers of the 1967 Disney adaptation of *The Jungle Book* wanted to use the voices of the four Beatles for what creatures? Unfortunately, they were turned down.
Q10. Who narrates the Harry Potter books in the UK version?

Round 3
Animal eyes
Name these creatures from their eyes

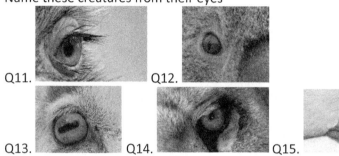

Q11.   Q12.

Q13.   Q14.   Q15.

Round 4
Another Queen round, sort of
This round is all about other queens and queens who are not real queens. Perhaps there should also be a round on how many times you can squeeze the word QUEEN into one sentence. You'll see what I mean

Q16. What Queen has the postcode E20 6PG?
Q17. Olivia Colman won an Oscar for her portrayal of what queen?
Q18. Bon Jovi had a hit called *Queen of* _____. Of where?
Q19. Marie Antoinette was a queen. What was her nationality?
Q20. Only one actor has portrayed both Queen Elizabeth I and Queen Elizabeth II in film. Who is she?

Round 5
Question of Sport – Mystery guests
Who are these sportspeople?

Q21.   Q22.

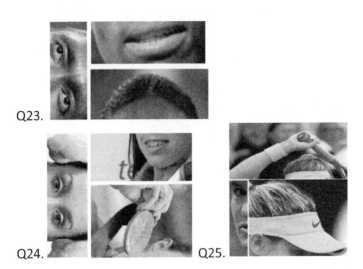

Q23.

Q24.

Q25.

Round 6
Connections

Q26. What do the films *The Shining*, *Key Largo* and *Pretty Woman* all have in common?

Q27. What country invented the game *Snakes and Ladders*?

Q28. Maggie Riley sings *Moonlight Shadow*, but who wrote and is credited as the lead artist?

Q29. Where do Humphrey Bogart and Walter Huston search for treasure in the 1948 movie?

Q30. Grandpa Joe and Grandpa George feature in which Roald Dahl book?

Q31. Which South American capital city has the fewest letters?

Q32. So, what's the connection?

QUIZ No. 44

Round 1
Famous opening lines
Q1. What famous Number One song opens with the lines,

'Sometimes you're better off dead

There's a gun in your hand and it's pointing at your head'?

Q2. What famous film opens with the line,

'It was the summer of 1963, when everybody called me Baby and it didn't occur to me to mind'?

Q3. What famous work of literature opens with the line,

'Call me Ishmael'?

Q4. What famous work of literature opens with the line

'It was a bright cold day in April, and the clocks were striking thirteen.'

Q5. What famous film opens with the line,

'Choose Life. Choose a job. Choose a career. Choose a family. Choose a f***ing big television.'

Round 2
Failed relationships
Here are questions about famous people, real and fictional, who have divorced.

Q6. What couple famously referred to their divorce as 'conscious uncoupling'?

Q7. Name the film director and pop star who married in 2000 and had a child called Rocco. They divorced after almost eight years together.

Q8. Who served divorce papers on whom on Christmas Day 1986, watched by more than 30 million people?

Q9. What famous couple married twice, first in 1964, the marriage lasting ten years, and then in 1975, that time lasting only one year?

Q10. A bloke called Andrew divorced his wife in 1995. They have a son called Tom. Andrew went on to marry a woman called Rosemary in 1996. The woman he divorced in 1995 is far more famous than either Andrew or Rosemary. Who is she?

Round 3
Statues and monuments

Q11. Where are these statues located?

Q12. What is the name of this memorial?

Q13. This is called The Motherland Calls. In what city would you find it?

Q14. To whom is this small monument dedicated?

Q15. Name this statue and the sculptor.

Round 4
Tools and equipment
Q16. What type of tool can be bench, croquet or Timmy?
Q17. What is the proper name of the profession that would use a hoop driver?
Q18. What piece of equipment has a feed dog, a take-up lever and a tension disk?
Q19. A shucker is most often used for opening what?
Q20. What traditional tradesperson would use a sack shutter, spar hook and a leggett paddle?

Round 5
Famous structures from unusual angles
Give the name of the structure.

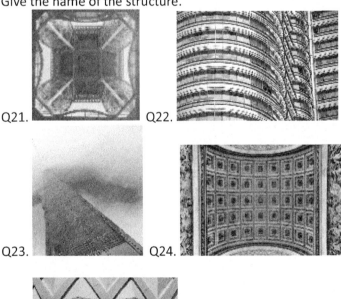

Q21.   Q22.

Q23.   Q24.

Q25.

Round 6

Connections

Q26. Who wrote the novel with the central characters Ralph, Jack, Simon, Piggy, Roger, Sam and Eric?

Q27. You've all seen the film *Notting Hill*, I assume. There is a scene in the film where Hugh Grant suggests that Julia Roberts would be good in a period drama by a particular American author, whose novels, interestingly, focus on Americans adapting to British life. The couple later meet again on Hampstead Heath, where Julia Roberts's character is filming a period drama by this very author. Name that author.

Q28. What is the name of the author who created the fictional detective Vera Stanhope?

Q29. What film and musical adaptation of a famous book includes the songs *Jolly Holiday* and *Fidelity Fiduciary Bank*?

Q30. A bloke with the surname Pennyworth is the unassuming butler to a famous character in film. We know him best by his first name. What is it?

Q31. Which of the seven natural wonders of the world is found on the border of Zimbabwe with Zambia?

Q32. So, what's the connection?

QUIZ No. 45

Round 1
Time

Q1. According to naval tradition, when the sun is over the yardarm, which equates to approximately 11 a.m., what are sailors allowed to do?

Q2. You all know that Russia is the world's largest country, but how many time zones does it span?

Q3. How many hours ahead or behind London is Lisbon?

Q4. Which famous Madonna hit, sampling Abba's classic *Gimme! Gimme! Gimme!*, begins with the lines,

> 'Time goes by so slowly, time goes by so slowly...'?

Q5. At precisely 2.20 a.m. on a cold April morning, the *Parisian*, *Verandah* and *Palm Court* cafes all closed for business and never reopened. Why?

Round 2
Missing words from famous speeches

Q6. From Jesus's sermon on the mount, give me the next four words:

> 'Blessed are the meek: for they ___ ___ ___ ___'.

Q7. This famous speech is best known by its first four words. It continues,

> 'One day this nation will rise up and live out the true meaning of its creed: we hold these truths to be self-evident, that all men are created equal.'

So, what are those first four words?

Q8. The most famous line of Winston Churchill's 'We shall fight them on the beaches' speech goes like this:

> 'We shall fight on the beaches, we shall fight on the landing grounds, we shall fight in the fields and in the streets, we shall fight _____.' Where else?

Q9. Iain Duncan Smith, when Tory leader, made a famous speech at the party conference, where he said,

'Do not underestimate the determination of a _____ man.'
What's the missing word?

Q10. This last one is not so much a speech as a quote. Complete this famous quote by Albert Einstein:

'I have no special talent. I am only passionately _____'.
What is the missing word?

Round 3
Venn diagrams
Give the middle part of each Venn diagram.

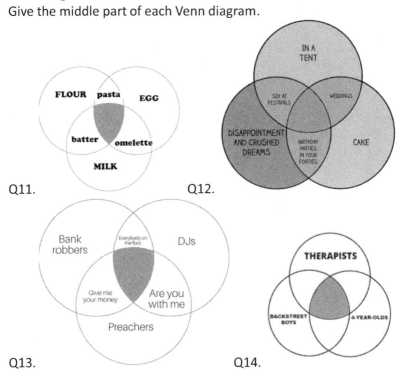

Q11.

Q12.

Q13.

Q14.

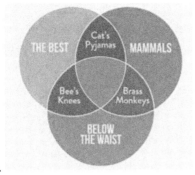

Q15.

Round 4
Anagrams of countries and capitals
The following are anagrams of countries and their capitals. See how you get on with these.

Q16. ALSATIAN A BRA CURER is an anagram of a country and its capital city. Name them both

Q17. A CARROT COMBO is an anagram of a country and its capital city. Name them both

Q18. BERLIN CUPBOARD NULLIFIED is an anagram of a country and its capital city. Name them both

Q19. ARABIC ZERO TAG is an anagram of a country and its capital city. Name them both

Q20. LEGO ATOM is an anagram of a country and its capital city. Name them both

Round 5
British seaside resorts
Q21. The modern building in the centre of the picture is the Turner Contemporary. But where is it?

169

Q22. Here is a picture of Sting in *Quadrophenia*. In what seaside resort is that film set?

Q23. The big building is Bleak House, on which Dickens based his novel of the same name. Dickens lived for a time in this seaside town. What is it called?

Q24. This seaside resort is also known as the surfing capital of the UK. Where is it?

Q25. This last seaside resort is also the name of a sitcom, the stars of which are pictured. What is its name?

Round 6
Connections
Q26. King Canute, the late World Darts Champion Andy Fordham and actor Travis Fimmel have what in common?
Q27. What word follows Lemon, Rock and Dover?
Q28. What popular alcoholic beverage is available in Original, Mint, Eton Mess, Orange Truffle, Salted Caramel and Tiramisu Cocktail flavours?
Q29. Newport is the principal town on what island?
Q30. All four Beatles were born in which decade?
Q31. David Walliams swam 140 miles for charity in 2011 along the length of what?
Q32. So, what's the connection?

QUIZ No. 46

Round 1
In the news
(10 October 2022)

Q1. The award-winning rapper Coolio died just recently. He was most famous for his smash hit *Gangsta's Paradise*, which was the theme to the film *Dangerous Minds*. What Hollywood star played the lead role in that famous film?

Q2. This week, Dave Gahan and Martin Gore announced they would be continuing to write and perform despite the recent death of fellow founding member Andy Fletcher. But of what famous group am I talking?

Q3. The Royal Mint has just unveiled the first coin design to depict King Charles III. What is the denomination of that coin?

Q4. The American Hans Niemann has been openly accused by other players of cheating, particularly by the current world champion, an accusation he continues to deny despite mounting evidence. In what sport is Niemann accused of cheating?

Q5. The most popular girls' and boys' names in the UK for 2022 have been released, and for the sixth year running, Olivia is the most popular girl's name. But what biblical name now tops the list of most popular boys' names in the UK?

Round 2
Sequences
I will give you a list of items; you tell me what comes next.

Q6. Trace, Williams, West, Singleton, _____?

Q7. King's Cross St. Pancras, Euston, Warren Street, Oxford Circus, Green Park _____?

Q8. Ramsey, Coggan, Runcie, Carey, Williams _____?

Q9. 1, 2, 5, 14, 41 ___?

Q10. 47, 53, 59, 61, 67 ___?

Round 3
Eating out

Here are some menus. All you have to do is tell me the name of the restaurant.

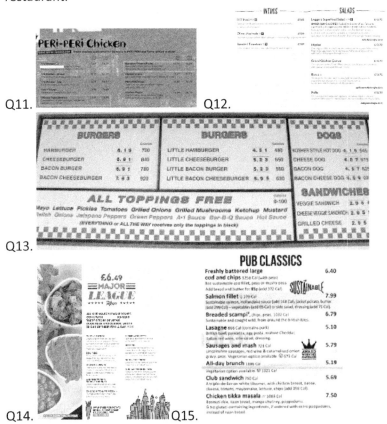

Q11.

Q12.

Q13.

Q14.

Q15.

Round 4
The Jane round

My sister Jane has a birthday on 14th October, so this round is dedicated to Janes.

Q16. Song lyric time. Minus the first word of the song, who sings the song that opens with,

'_____ Jane, don't leave me hanging on the line'?

Q17. Which Bond girl actress shares her name and surname with a Queen?

Q18. What is the first name of the central character with the surname Jane, in the TV series *The Mentalist*?

Q19. What is the surname of the famous actor Henry, who had a famous actor daughter called Jane?

Q20. What famous Jane said, 'The person, be it gentleman or lady, who has not pleasure in a good novel, must be intolerably stupid'?

Round 5
Sketches of famous buildings

Q21. This castle is in England. Its name would seem to be a little inappropriate. Where is it?

Q22. This is the Customs House, and it stands on the river running through a capital city. What is that capital city?

Q23. This is a famous government building in Europe. What is it called?

Q24. This is one of Europe's largest and most famous opera houses. What is it called?

Q25. Here is a railway station in the Midlands. Where is it?

Round 6
Connections

Q26. What word comes before Davies, Knot and Castle?

Q27. The writer Oscar Wilde wrote a famous poem-ballad that bears the name of the place where he was incarcerated. So, what was the name of the place where Oscar Wilde was imprisoned?

Q28. Complete this famous foursome: Randy Meisner, Bernie Leadon, Glenn Frey...

Q29. The poet Matthew Arnold gave what city the moniker 'the city of dreaming spires'?

Q30. What fictional detective first appeared in the 1939 novel *The Big Sleep*?

Q31. What city is found both on the Humber and in the Caribbean?

Q32. So, what's the connection?

QUIZ No. 47

Round 1
Compass points
The answers to these questions will be one of North, South, East or West. None of those north-north-west shenanigans. And all the answers are based on 'as the crow flies'.

Q1. If I travel from Leeds to Sheffield, in which direction will I travel?

Q2. If I travel from Corsica to Sardinia, in which direction will I travel?

Q3. If I travel from Antwerp to The Hague, in which direction will I travel?

Q4. If I travel from Luton Airport to Stansted Airport, in which direction will I travel?

Q5. If I travel from Chicago to Detroit, in which direction will I travel?

Round 2
Miscellaneous sport
Q6. In what sport is the men's world record 74m, but the women's world record is almost 77m?

Q7. The terms BOSS, FLEX, NOCK and VANE are used in what sport?

Q8. A swimmer from Equatorial Guinea who had never seen, let alone swim, in an Olympic swimming pool won his heat in the 100m freestyle in the slowest ever time recorded for the event. What was the nickname he was given?

Q9. What do the Olympic achievements of Richard Thompson of Trinidad and Tobago in 2008, Yohan Blake of Jamaica in 2012 and Justin Gatlin of the USA in 2016 all have in common?

Q10. A 240-odd-kilometre race between two cities has been held since 1983 to mark the achievement of a long-distance runner who ran the distance to announce victory in the Battle of Marathon before promptly dropping dead. His feat inspired the modern marathon race, but my question is this: between which two cities is this race run? Half a point for each.

Round 3
Minimalist film posters

Can you work out the following films from the minimalist posters that I have created? As a clue, I will give you the colours, where appropriate.

Q11. (Yellow background)

Q12. (Red background)

Q13.

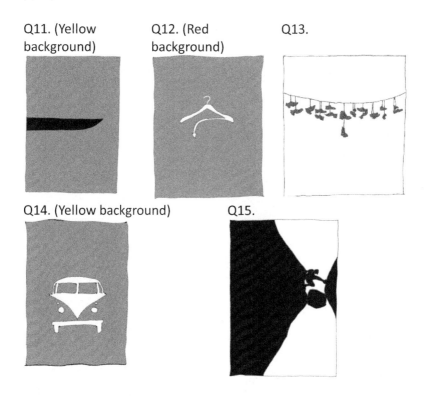

Q14. (Yellow background)

Q15.

Round 4
Banksy

Q16. You all remember the incident at auction when a famous Banksy picture was shredded when it sold. What did that picture depict?

Q17. Banksy's famous work *Mild Mild West* features who or what throwing a Molotov Cocktail at the police?

Q18. Celebrating superhero NHS workers during the pandemic, Banksy produced a piece that first appeared in a foyer at Southampton General Hospital. It depicts a small boy playing with a toy nurse superhero doll while two other superhero dolls are discarded in a waste bin. One of those superheroes is Batman. Who is the other?

Q19. Banksy is thought to hail from which British city? At least, there are more Banksy works here than anywhere else.

Q20. Banksy created a dystopian theme park featuring such models as a crashed Cinderella pumpkin carriage, a derelict castle and a killer whale jumping out of a toilet. What is it called?

Round 5
Famous walls
Name the famous walls. For Q24., tell me who owns it.

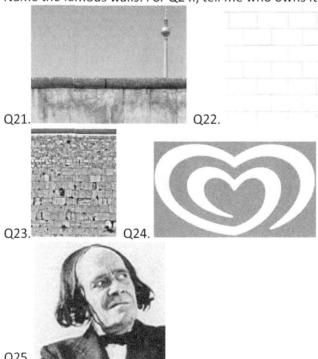

Q21.   Q22.

Q23.   Q24.

Q25.

Round 6
Connections

Q26. What is the name of the 2013 to 2017 TV series which is advertised as a contemporary prequel to the film *Psycho*?

Q27. What franchise features 922 fictional species, including Charmander, Squirtle and Bulbasaur?

Q28. The films *Dangal* and *Secret Superstar* are two of the highest-grossing films from what particular industry?

Q29. What is the name of the device that is used by law-enforcement officers where a chemical reaction sees the reddish-orange-coloured potassium dichromate ion change to the green-coloured chromium ion?

Q30. What 5-letter word is a substance used to relax the muscles in your face to smooth out lines and wrinkles?

Q31. *Monty Python and the Holy Grail* was rewritten as a musical comedy. What is it called?

Q32. So, what's the connection?

QUIZ No. 48

Round 1
Driving on British roads

Q1. The Gravelly Hill Interchange is Junction 6 of the M6 motorway, at the point where it meets the A38(M). By what name is this interchange more popularly known?

Q2. What do Krone, Montracon and Lawrence David manufacture? I guarantee that you have seen these names when driving on Britain's roads.

Q3. You know that brown signs on British roads indicate places of interest. If you see a brown sign with the white image of a bull's head on it, to what kind of place of interest would that sign be directing you?

Q4. Some might say that the A308(M) in Berkshire holds this particular title, but I think the title should actually go to the A635(M) in Manchester. What title am I talking about?

Q5. Some road-based arithmetic to end the round. Add the number of the highest motorway in the UK above sea level to the number of the busiest motorway in the UK. What do you get?

Round 2
Coronation Street anagrams

Someone asked for *Coronation Street*, and to make it a little more accessible to non-soap fans, I am levelling the playing field by making this an anagram round.

Q6. INTERCITY MAN is an anagram of the character played by Michelle Keegan. Name that character.

Q7. ANNE SENT RIND is an anagram of a character who returned to Corrie after an absence of 43 years. What is that character's name?

Q8. Between 1960 and 1965, the actor Arthur Lowe, famous, of course, for his role in *Dad's Army*, played which character, whose name is an anagram of NORWAY NEEDS LIDL?

Q9. DENVER HAWKS TIGHTENED is an anagram of which monarch? In the soap's fictional history, the street was named in honour of that monarch's coronation.

Q10. GUNPOWDER SKYJACKED CRUTCH is an anagram of two people who both worked on *Coronation Street* as lollipop men. Give me both their names (names and surnames). No half points.

Round 3
Formula 1 Grand Prix circuits on maps

Q11. Name the Formula 1 track on the map.

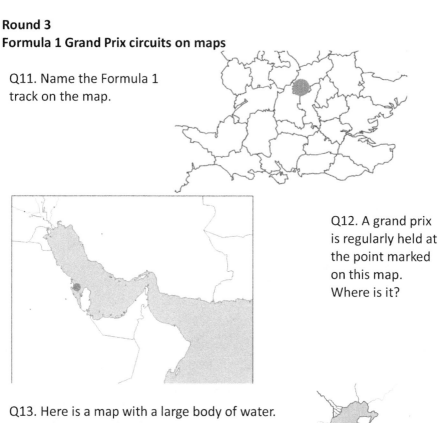

Q12. A grand prix is regularly held at the point marked on this map. Where is it?

Q13. Here is a map with a large body of water. Name the city marked by the dot where a grand prix is held.

Q14. Name the grand prix marked by the dot on this map.

Q15. I have blocked out a country that hosts a regular grand prix. Name the country.

Round 4
Cryptic film and book titles
Q16. Integer Travelled Fast Above Home For Unwelcome Guest
Q17. Men You Can't Put Your Finger On
Q18. Map of Nimbi
Q19. Bird of Prey From the Mediterranean
Q20. Charlie and the Scottish River

Round 5
Fortresses and castles

Q21. What is the name of this fictional castle?

Q22. This palace forms part of a famous fortress complex. What is the complex called?

Q23. What is the name of this castle?

Q24. What is the precise name of this castle?

Q25. What is the name of this castle?

183

Round 6

Connections

Q26. Who wrote the famous piece of classical music that begins with *La Primavera* and ends with *L'Inverno*?

Q27. You have heard of Alfred the Great and Ethelred the Unready as famous kings of England. However, what name is shared by the monarch 'The Elder' in the late 9th century and 'The Martyr' in the 10th century?

Q28. The wife of King George III shares her name with the capital of the US state of North Carolina. What name is that?

Q29. CARDIGAN ELEVEN is an anagram of what famous model and actor?

Q30. What is the name of the musical biography of The Four Seasons?

Q31. What was the name of the oil platform about 120 miles from Aberdeen in the North Sea that exploded and sank in July 1988?

Q32. So, what's the connection?

QUIZ No. 49

Round 1
Witches
Q1. What is the name of the witch in *Sleeping Beauty*, recently recreated by Angelina Jolie in the film of the same name?

Q2. Susan Sarandon, Michelle Pfeiffer and Cher played three witches from what town?

Q3. Samantha Stephens is a housewife and witch in what famous sitcom?

Q4. What is the name of the witch played by Maggie Smith in the Harry Potter stories?

Q5. GREENHORN MIRAGE is an anagram of what famous witch?

Round 2
General knowledge with arithmetic
Q6. Add the first Apollo mission to land humans on the Moon to the number of stripes on the US flag.

Q7. Take the number of blocks Bruce Willis had to accompany a prisoner to safety and subtract that from Paul Hardcastle's most famous song.

Q8. Multiply the number of players in a rugby union team by the number of a cat's lives.

Q9. Divide the Internet 'page not found' code by the number of dogs in Dodie Smith's famous book.

Q10. Add the following together:
The highest number on a roulette wheel, the number of original members of the Monkees and the number that corresponds to MNO on a telephone keypad.

Round 3
Biscuits

These drawings are all to scale.

Q11. Name the biscuit from my drawing. I have removed the words that appear in the centre

Q12. Name this biscuit from the pattern

Q13. This one is to scale, including the ten dots. The marks in the centre are parts of lettering.

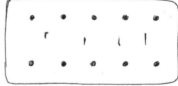

Q14. This is a to-scale drawing of another favourite. I have left part of the lettering in as a clue.

Q15. Also to scale

Round 4
More words from the Periodic Table

For example, if I say Fluorine, Uranium and Nitrogen, you get F+U+N= FUN. Which this round promises to be, right?

Q16. Silicon+Molybdenum+Nitrogen
Q17. Phosphorus+Hydrogen+Yttrium+Silicon+Caesium
Q18. Actinium+Copper+Radium+Carbon+Yttrium
Q19. Germanium+Nickel+Uranium+Sulphur
Q20. Helium+Lithium+Cobalt+Platinum+Erbium

Round 5
Famous assassinations

Q21. Who was assassinated in one of these? It's a 1961 Lincoln Continental convertible if you're interested.

Q22. Here is a police artist's sketch of a famous assassination. Who was the victim?

Q23. Who was assassinated on the balcony of this motel?

Q24. This shrine is made of three swords and stands at the site of a famous assassination. To whom was the shrine erected?

Q25. Name the assassination victim whose work featured prominently in these productions.

Round 6
Connections
Q26. What is the first name of the lead singer of the band Bon Jovi?

Q27. What word is the surname of snooker player David and the grape played by Jonny Depp?

Q28. What famous scientist appears on the new polymer £50 note?

Q29. Kenneth Branagh, Emma Thompson, Denzel Washington and Keanu Reeves all starred in a Hollywood adaptation of which Shakespeare play?

Q30. Who has played a black widow, nutmeg, Lucy and Mary Boleyn?

Q31. In diving, there are four principal positions. Free, Straight and Pike are three. What is the fourth?

Q32. So, what's the connection?

QUIZ No. 50

Round 1
50 is L in Roman numerals
The answers to the following questions all begin with the letter L.

Q1. What is the name of the cyclist who won seven Tour de France titles only to have them all taken away for being a very naughty boy?

Q2. What is the name of the famous British ocean liner that was launched in 1906 by Cunard but was torpedoed by a German U-boat and sunk during the First World War?

Q3. What art-world structure is a little over 21 metres tall and contains approximately 670 glass segments?

Q4. A church that sits atop the Mount of Olives in Jerusalem has ceramic-tiled reproductions of what, in over 140 different languages of the world?

Q5. What is the surname of the President of Belarus?

Round 2
50-50
One or the other. If you don't know the answer, you can guess.

Q6. Is the town of Ypres in France or Belgium?

Q7. Was it the Brothers Grimm or Hans Christian Anderson who wrote *The Princess and the Pea*?

Q8. Was it Westlife or Boyzone who sang the song *Queen of My Heart*?

Q9. Celtic or Rangers – which team has won the Scottish Football League the most?

Q10. Who hosted the most shows in *University Challenge* – Bamber Gascoigne or Jeremy Paxman?

Round 3
Beer

Here are labels from famous breweries, only with the name removed. Your job? Name the brands. Come on, boozers, how hard can this be?

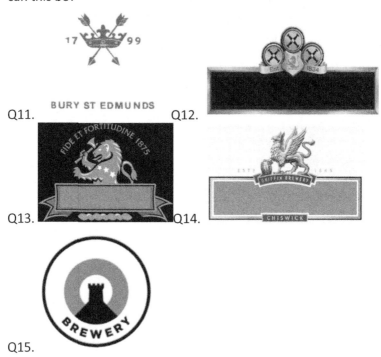

Q11.

Q12.

Q13.

Q14.

Q15.

Round 4
The Answer is 50

This is a basic addition round; you have to give the two numbers that make 50 in the correct order based on the following questions. For example, if I ask you what a bullseye is worth in darts and how many times I have won the world darts championships, your answer should be 50 + 0 = 50.

Q16. What number features in the title of the John Buchan novel about Richard Hannay, AND what number featured in the title of the film when George Clooney first got a band of blokes together to rob Andy Garcia's casinos?

Q17. How many UK number-one singles did the Spice Girls have, AND in what year did the USA join in World War Two (last two digits)?

Q18. How many states are there in India, AND how many yards are there in a chain?

Q19. What is the country dialling code for Austria, AND what was Andriy Shevchenko's shirt number at Chelsea and AC Milan?

Q20. How old was Roger Federer when he won his last Grand Slam title, AND which amendment of the United States Constitution grants all persons born or naturalised in the United States equal protection of the law?

Round 5
50% faces
Name these people from the 50% of their faces shown. One of these might prove tricky if you haven't been paying attention.

Q21.

Q22.

Q23.
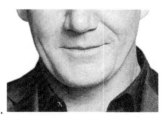
Q24.

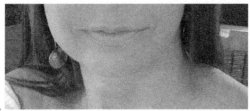

Q25.

Round 6
Connections

Q26. What is the former name of Sri Lanka?

Q27. What model car replaced the Zephyr and was known in Europe as the Consul?

Q28. In what city were 11 Israeli athletes murdered at a major sporting event?

Q29. What name was given to a demonstration of Roman Catholic civil rights protestors in Londonderry that turned violent after British paratroopers opened fire?

Q30. What is the name of the Welsh boxer who retired in 2009 with 46 wins from 46 fights?

Q31. Who was the first Briton in space as part of the European Space Agency?

Q32. So, what's the connection?

ANSWERS

Quiz No. 1

Round 1
Q1. Anton Chekhov
Q2. Datsun
Q3. Banks (That's the family in *Mary Poppins*)
Q4. Queen Anne
Q5. Lambert (as in Lambert and Butler)

Round 2
Q6. Little John
Q7. Loxley
Q8. Alan A'Dale
Q9. Mighty
Q10. Will Scarlet

Round 3
Q11. Menai Bridge
Q12. *The Bridges of Madison County*
Q13. *Bridge of Spies*
Q14. *The Bridge on the River Kwai*
Q15. *The Big Lebowski*

Round 4
Q16. Serbian
Q17. Sabre
Q18. Hublot
Q19. Phil Taylor
Q20. Snooker

Round 5
Q21. Sudan—Japan
Q22. Isle of Man—Cannes
Q23. Ukraine—Bahrain
Q24. Gambia—Zambia
Q25. Mozambique—Martinique

Round 6
Q26. Snow White
Q27. Chris Martin (named his daughter Apple)
Q28. Newton
Q29. Rossini (William Tell)
Q30. The first name Adam
Q31. Strudel
Q32. APPLE

Quiz No. 2

Round 1
Q1. *The Chronicles of Narnia*
Q2. *Meg & Mog*
Q3. *Psycho*
Q4. *Ghostbusters*
Q5. Smashing Pumpkins

Round 2
Q6. Ringo (The Beatles)
Q7. L for fifty
Q8. 64
Q9. 6 (next number clockwise on a dartboard)
Q10. DC (Daniel Craig) — James Bond actors

Round 3
Q11. *Driving Miss DAISY*
Q12. Alec Guinness (*The LAVENDER Hill Mob*)
Q13. Moaning MYRTLE
Q14. *The GRAPES of Wrath*
Q15. *Steel MAGNOLIAS*

Round 4
Q16. Shirley Williams
Q17. Sir Ed Davey
Q18. Theresa MAY
Q19. David Lloyd George
Q20. ...have been murdered in office

Round 5
Q21. Donald and Kiefer Sutherland
Q22. Hilary and Chelsea Clinton
Q23. Stellen and Alexander Skarsgard
Q24. Goldie Hawn and Kate Hudson
Q25. Jon Voight and Angelina Jolie

Round 6
Q26. *Guardians of the GALAXY*
Q27. River Plate
Q28. ROTOR
Q29. Sparta
Q30. Corinthians
Q31. Vasco de Gama
Q32. Football teams (LA Galaxy, River Plate (Argentina), ROTOR Volgograd (Russia), Sparta Prague (Czechia), Corinthians and Vasco de Gama (Brazil))

Quiz No. 3

Round 1
Q1. *Blue Monday* (New Order)
Q2. *Golden Brown* (The Stranglers)
Q3. *Gold* (Spandau Ballet)
Q4. *Red Right Hand* (Nick Cave)
Q5. *White Flag* (Dido)

Round 2
Q6. St Elmo's Fire
Q7. Nero
Q8. *Chariots of Fire*
Q9. Pudding Lane
Q10. Red Adair

Round 3
Q11. Clint Eastwood on Vincent Van Gogh
Q12. Uma Thurman on Botticelli's Venus
Q13. Pablo Picasso on Wolfgang Amadeus Mozart
Q14. Albert Einstein on George Washington
Q15. Freddie Mercury on Freda Kahlo

Round 4
Q16. Badminton
Q17. Whiff Whaff
Q18. Squash
Q19. The fastest serve (163.4 mph)
Q20. Croatia

Round 5
Q21. Arc de Triomphe
Q22. Wellington Arch
Q23. Berlin
Q24. The Unknown Warrior
Q25. Danube

Round 6
Q26. Usain BOLT
Q27. Wings
Q28. Windows
Q29. Speaker
Q30. Florida KEYS
Q31. They are all TRIANGLES
Q32. The answers are all parts of an automobile

Quiz No. 4

Round 1
Q1. Screwdriver
Q2. Sidecar
Q3. Negroni
Q4. Ian Fleming
Q5. Cranberry juice

Round 2
Q6. W (George W Bush)
Q7. J
Q8. C
Q9. S
Q10. Q (James Bond films)

Round 3
Q11. Library of Congress
Q12. North Korea
Q13. Saudi Arabia (Mecca)
Q14. St Peter's Basilica, Rome
Q15. Synagogue (Israel)

Round 4
Q16. Gdansk
Q17. Capital city
Q18. Frédéric Chopin
Q19. Vodka
Q20. A castle

Round 5
Q21. Lexus
Q22. Bugatti
Q23. Alfa Romeo
Q24. Morgan
Q25. BMW

Round 6
Q26. Bows
Q27. North and South CIRCULAR
Q28. A chain
Q29. Frets
Q30. Jig
Q31. Mitre
Q32. The answers are all types of saw

Quiz No. 5

Round 1
Q1. Baseball
Q2. Ice Skating
Q3. James Hunt and Niki Lauda
Q4. *The Hustler*
Q5. Chess

Round 2
Q6. Topic
Q7. Yorkie
Q8. Quality Street
Q9. Snickers
Q10. Bounty

Round 3
Q11. Skywalker
Q12. Addams
Q13. Nazi Party
Q14. Mexico
Q15. Prince of Wales

Round 4
Q16. Hamster
Q17. Princes William and Harry
Q18. Luis Suarez
Q19. Crimean War
Q20. Super Caley Go Ballistic, Celtic are Atrocious

Round 5
Q21. Graceland (home of Elvis Presley)
Q22. Norwich
Q23. The Élysée Palace
Q24. Sandringham
Q25. Ernest Hemingway

Round 6
Q26. DoppleGANGer
Q27. *Super TROOPer*, by Abba
Q28. Antonio BANDeras
Q29. VaSECTomies
Q30. BatMOBile
Q31. sCREWfix
Q32. The answers all contain words for a group of people

Quiz No. 6

Round 1
Q1. Frostbite
Q2. Tinsellitis
Q3. Deep-pan, crisp and even
Q4. He had nobody to go with
Q5. They had a weigh in a manger

Round 2
Q6. Hawaii
Q7. Chile
Q8. Cotopaxi
Q9. Lake Baikal
Q10. Dhaka, Bangladesh

Round 3
Q11. Lionel Messi
Q12. Ursula Von Der Leyen
Q13. Ronnie O'Sullivan
Q14. Prince George
Q15. Greta Thunberg

Round 4
Q16. Greece
Q17. Jambalaya
Q18. Georgia
Q19. Sweden
Q20. Goulash

Round 5
Q21. What goes up must come down
Q22. *The League of Gentlemen*
Q23. *The Full Monty*
Q24. *Dances With Wolves*
Q25. *The Boys Are Back In Town*

Round 6
Q26. Walker
Q27. Stanley
Q28. Jacket (No Jacket Required)
Q29. King George V
Q30. Field
Q31. Yellow
Q32. The answers all contain the name of a famous sporting trophy
Walker Cup (golf), Stanley Cup (ice hockey), Green Jacket (US Open golf), King George V Gold Cup (Horseracing), Field Cup (Wimbledon - Men), Yellow jersey (Tour de France)

Quiz No. 7

Round 1
Q1. East 17
Q2. Renee and Renato
Q3. The Flying Pickets
Q4. *Ernie, the Fastest Milkman in the West*
Q5. *Sound of the Underground*

Round 2
Q6. PIE HARD/DIE HARD
Q7. HOVE ACTUALLY/LOVE ACTUALLY
Q8. IT'S A WONDERFUL LIFE/LIME
Q9. COME ALONE/HOME ALONE
Q10. A CHRISTMAS CAROL/CAREL

Round 3
Q11. Corgi's bottom
Q12. 5
Q13. Labradoodles
Q14. Fried chicken
Q15. 5

Round 4
Q16. A question mark followed by an exclamation mark (?!)
Q17. A beetle
Q18. Ice hockey puck
Q19. Unicorns
Q20. Spock (Star Trek)

Round 5
Q21. Brad Pitt is the odd one out because the other three have all played Batman in the movies
Q22. Ariana Grande is the odd one out. The other three have the same name as members of the royal family (MEGHAN Trainor, HARRY Styles and DIANA Ross)
Q23. The odd one out is Canterbury Cathedral (the bottom-right picture). The others are all minsters (Southwell Minster, York Minster, Beverley Minster)
Q24. The odd one out is CELERY. The other three are all classed as fruits (cucumber, avocado and okra)
Q25. Picture 3 is the odd one out, as the matches in this one don't make two rectangles

Round 6
Q26. Last
Q27. Heart
Q28. Very
Q29. Next
Q30. DAY
Q31. Tears
Q32. The words all appear in the first part of Wham's *Last Christmas*

201

Quiz No. 8

Round 1
Q1. *White Christmas*
Q2. *Frosty the Snowman*
Q3. *Hark the Herald Angels Sing*
Q4. *It's Beginning to Look a Lot Like Christmas*
Q5. *The First Noel*

Round 2
Q6. Mistletoe
Q7. Holly
Q8. Norway
Q9. Poinsettia
Q10. Cloves

Round 3
Q11. *Elf*
Q12. *Nightmare Before Christmas*
Q13. *Arthur Christmas*
Q14. *The Holiday*
Q15. *Home Alone*

Round 4
Q16. Seven swans a-swimming
Q17. Donald Trump
Q18. *The Polar Express*
Q19. Great Britain
Q20. Germany

Round 5
Q21. Noel
Q22. Opening presents
Q23. Mints Pies (Mince Pies)
Q24. *The Grinch Who Stole Christmas*
Q25. Wrapping paper

Round 6
Q26. Bread
Q27. Brussels
Q28. Turkey
Q29. Pig
Q30. Cranberries
Q31. Professor Plum
Q32. The answers are all elements of a traditional Christmas dinner

Quiz No. 9

Round 1
Q1. Ed Sheeran and Elton John
Q2. The Beatles
Q3. Samuel Pepys
Q4. 1964
Q5. Ellis Island

Round 2
Q6. Connect 4
Q7. Secret Hitler
Q8. Backgammon
Q9. LUDO
Q10. Boggle

Round 3
Q11. *Silence of the Lambs*
Q12. *Scarface*
Q13. *The Godfather*
Q14. *American Beauty*
Q15. *The Exorcist*

Round 4
Q16. *Captain America*
Q17. *Les Miserables*
Q18. *Dambusters*
Q19. *Wall-E*
Q20. *Lion King*

Round 5
Q21. Boston Red Sox
Q22. Chicago Bulls
Q23. Sporting Lisbon
Q24. Everton
Q25. Pittsburgh Penguins

Round 6
Q26. The SUN
Q27. His DRAGON
Q28. The GEORGE CROSS
Q29. STAR
Q30. KALASHNIKOV
Q31. MAPLE
Q32. They are all things that appear on flags of the world

Quiz No. 10

Round 1
Q1. Bashful
Q2. Pocahontas
Q3. *Ratatouille*
Q4. Peter Pan
Q5. Left

Round 2
Q6. Japan
Q7. Israel
Q8. Finland or Sweden
Q9. Tortellini
Q10. Samosa

Round 3
Q11. Sophie Raworth / Peter Snow
Q12. Dastardly and Muttley
Q13. Paul Newman / Robert Redford
Q14. Sonny and Cher
Q15. Neil and Glenys Kinnock

Round 4
Q16. HG Wells
Q17. DH Lawrence
Q18. KD Lang
Q19. E Nesbit (*Railway Children*)
Q20. L Ron Hubbard

Round 5
Q21. Manx
Q22. Scottish Fold
Q23. Jaguar
Q24. Bengal
Q25. Maine Coon

Round 6
Q26. Tom CLANCY
Q27. GLASTONBURY
Q28. WHITBY
Q29. Michael BOLTON
Q30. WESTMINSTER Palace
Q31. Grand NATIONAL
Q32. ABBEYs

Quiz No. 11

Round 1
Q1. Edward Jenner
Q2. The Pythagorean Theorem
Q3. Stephen Hawking
Q4. The GOD Particle
Q5. Grantham

Round 2
Q6. Antonio da Cividale was an Italian composer from the early Renaissance.
Q7. Michele Pesenti (1470–1524) was an Italian composer and lute player.
Q8. Pasta. Bigoli is an extruded pasta in the form of a long and thick strand.
Q9. Pasta. Sagnarelli is a type of ribbon pasta. They are typically rectangular ribbons with fluted edges.
Q10. Composer. Luigi Dentice was an Italian composer from the 16th century

Round 3
Q11. Andre Agassi
Q12. Moby
Q13. Patrick Stewart
Q14. Bernie Sanders
Q15. Vin Diesel

Round 4
Q16. *Orange is the New Black*
Q17. *The Color Purple*
Q18. *Crimson and Clover* (Tommy James and the Shondells)
Q19. *White Teeth* (Zadie Smith)
Q20. *I Can Sing A Rainbow*

Round 5
Q21. Michael Johnson
Q22. Zola Pieterse (was Zola Budd)
Q23. Tommy Smith
Q24. Ian Thorpe
Q25. Usain Bolt

Round 6
Q26. Tom
Q27. Oliver
Q28. Boys
Q29. Thomas
Q30. Fool
Q31. Robert
Q32. HARDY

Quiz No. 12

Round 1
Q1. Anne
Q2. 50 pence (Wine for £10.50, bag for £0.50)
Q3. He was walking
Q4. Helen is playing chess with Cherrie
Q5. He's playing Monopoly

Round 2
Q6. *The Last Mohican*
Q7. Go into space
Q8. Swim the channel unaided
Q9. Grace Kelly
Q10. Prince Edward and Sophie, Countess of Wessex

Round 3
Q11. The Shard
Q12. The Pentagon
Q13. Sicily and Italy
Q14. Taipei 101
Q15. Golden Gate Bridge

Round 4
Q16. *Friends*
Q17. *The Good, The Bad and The Ugly*
Q18. *Moon River*
Q19. *On Her Majesty's Secret Service*
Q20. *The Fall Guy*

Round 5
Q21. Pencil Sharpener
Q22. Bayonet light bulb fitting
Q23. Garlic
Q24. Digital display
Q25. Dartboard

Round 6
Q26. Mick JAGGER
Q27. OLIVER
Q28. *MARLEY and Me*
Q29. DAVID COPPERFIELD
Q30. PIPs
Q31. DODGERS
Q32. Characters from works by Charles Dickens

Quiz No. 13

Round 1
Q1. StationEry is paper, envelopes, paperclips etc. StationAry is standing still
Q2. A vegetable, also known as a German Turnip
Q3. It is a cosmodrome or space launch site located in Kazakhstan and used by Russia for all its space missions
Q4. Polystyrene
Q5. FILIBUSTERING

Round 2
Q6. C+O+Ac+H
Q7. Am+B+Er
Q8. Be+Er
Q9. Ta+N+K+Ar+D
Q10. Si+Mo+N

Round 3
Q11. Tilda Swinton
Q12. Robert DeNiro
Q13. Professor Chris Whitty, Chief Medical Officer
Q14. Siouxsie Su (Siouxsie and the Banshees)
Q15. Maggie Smith

Round 4
Q16. Edinburgh
Q17. Wigan
Q18. Norway
Q19. London Eye
Q20. Chile

Round 5
Q21. AHA, *Take on Me*
Q22. Peter Gabriel, *Sledgehammer*
Q23. Kety Perry, *Firework*
Q24. Billie Eilish, *Bad Guy*
Q25. David Bowie, *Let's Dance*

Round 6
Q26. Toothbrush
Q27. Horseshoe
Q28. Magnum (Champagne bottle sizes)
Q29. Pencils
Q30. Chevron
Q31. The Walrus
Q32. They are all types of MOUSTACHE

207

Quiz No. 14

Round 1
Q1. Eddie Redmayne
Q2. Tonsils
Q3. All Norwegian
Q4. Poet Laureate
Q5. Magna Carta

Round 2
Q6. The European Union
Q7. Nuclear weapons
Q8. Kensington
Q9. Stockholm
Q10. Berlin

Round 3
Q11. *Turner and Hooch*
Q12. Bolt
Q13. Beethoven
Q14. Toto
Q15. Tramp

Round 4
Q16. Belgium
Q17. Australia
Q18. Sweden
Q19. New Zealand
Q20. Monaco

Round 5
Q21. Pak Choi
Q22. Okra
Q23. Jerusalem artichokes
Q24. Rainbow chard
Q25. Buckwheat

Round 6
Q26. Grasshopper Zurich
Q27. Tennessee Williams
Q28. Scarlett Johanssen
Q29. Guerrilla
Q30. Jonny Depp
Q31. Raccoon
Q32. Two or more sets of double letters

Quiz No. 15

Round 1
Q1. Oysters
Q2. Padlocks
Q3. Atria (atrium) and ventricles
Q4. Dom Perignon
Q5. Mercury

Round 2
Q6. *Tainted Love* (Soft Cell)
Q7. *Love is All Around* (Wet Wet Wet)
Q8. *The Look of Love*
Q9. *ANOTHER Love*
Q10. *What Time is Love?* (KLF)

Round 3
Q11. *Pretty Woman*
Q12. *Two Weeks' Notice*
Q13. *Green Card*
Q14. *How to Lose a Guy in 10 Days*
Q15. *Bride and Prejudice*

Round 4
Q16. *Two Gentlemen of Verona*
Q17. *Shirley Valentine*
Q18. VALENTINE'S DAY MASSACRE
Q19. *My Funny Valentine*
Q20. Beekeepers

Round 5
Q21. *Notting Hill*
Q22. *The King's Speech*
Q23. *Sabrina*
Q24. *Sense and Sensibility*
Q25. *When Harry Met Sally*

Round 6
Q26. Pompidou Centre (in PARIS)
Q27. Helen of Troy (Brad Pitt played the bloke on the right, whose name is PARIS)
Q28. *Phantom of the Opera* (set in PARIS)
Q29. *Ratatouille* (set in PARIS_
Q30. The French Open (Roland Garros) (held in PARIS)
Q31. *Taken* (where Liam Neeson pretty much destroys PARIS to get his daughter back)
Q32. PARIS

Quiz No. 16

Round 1
Q1. *The Three Amigos*
Q2. Flour
Q3. GET OUT
Q4. Jean Valjean (Les Mis)
Q5. Charing Cross

Round 2
Q6. Tax Collector
Q7. Le Blanc and Perry
Q8. Groening
Q9. Bros
Q10. Broderick

Round 3
Q11. Usain Bolt
Q12. Anthony Hopkins
Q13. Tony Blair
Q14. Hillary Clinton
Q15. Colin Firth

Round 4
Q16. Curling
Q17. Jamaica
Q18. Norway (16 gold medals)
Q19. Ski jumping
Q20. Figure skating

Round 5
Q21. Mary Shelley
Q22. Coco Chanel
Q23. Margaret Atwood (author of The Handmaid's Tale)
Q24. Simone de Beauvoir
Q25. Climb Mount Everest

Round 6
Q26. RABIES
Q27. RAIN-man
Q28. PLANE
Q29. ENEMY
Q30. CHAIN
Q31. PURE and simple
Q32. The answers are all anagrams of countries (Serbia, Iran, Nepal, Yemen, China, Peru)

Quiz No. 17

Round 1
Q1. Cyprus
Q2. Lake Constance
Q3. Algiers
Q4. Rio Grande
Q5. San Francisco

Round 2
Q6. Drag queen
Q7. Racehorse
Q8. Drag queen
Q9. Racehorse
Q10. Racehorse

Round 3
Q11. *Blackadder*
Q12. *Fawlty Towers*
Q13. *Only Fools and Horses*
Q14. *The Good Life*
Q15. *Bread*

Round 4
Q16. Alexandre Dumas
Q17. Athos
Q18. Richelieu
Q19. Twenty
Q20. *Dogtanian and the Three Muskehounds*

Round 5
Q21. Harpsichord
Q22. Theremin
Q23. Piccolo
Q24. Bassoon
Q25. Sousaphone

Round 6
Q26. Malik
Q27. Corrie
Q28. Dudley
Q29. Eunice
Q30. Franklin
Q31. Gladys
Q32. The answers are the names of the storms that hit the UK in 2022

Quiz No. 18

Round 1
Q1. Mark Twain
Q2. The Trump presidency
Q3. Archduke Franz Ferdinand
Q4. Richard Burton
Q5. Presidents Lincoln and Kennedy

Round 2
Q6. Miss Marple
Q7. Maigret
Q8. Jim Rockford
Q9. Book 'em Danno
Q10. Dirk Gently

Round 3
Q11. Buckingham Palace
Q12. Cologne Cathedral
Q13. Brandenburg Gate
Q14. Bill Gates
Q15. Gareth Gates

Round 4
Q16. *Rain Man*
Q17. *A Beautiful Mind*
Q18. *Parasite*
Q19. *Slumdog Millionaire*
Q20. *Forrest Gump*

Round 5
Q21. Margaret Thatcher
Q22. Gordon Brown
Q23. Nicolas Sarkozy, former President of France
Q24. Jamie Oliver
Q25. Julia Roberts

Round 6
Q26. Taxi Driver
Q27. Lucy
Q28. Leon (Spinx)
Q29. Subway
Q30. Kamikazi
Q31. 5. Boron, the fifth element
Q32. Luc Besson

Quiz No. 19

Round 1
Q1. QUEEN – the only word that does not appear in the title of a Shakespeare play
Q2. They are all walled cities
Q3. SOMBRERO
Q4. MARYLEBONE – the fourth station in Monopoly
Q5. They are all towers you can find at the Tower of London

Round 2
Q6. *The Matrix*
Q7. *Grease*
Q8. *Home Alone*
Q9. *Cloudy With a Chance of Meatballs*
Q10. *Lost in Translation* (of course)

Round 3
Q11. Battenberg
Q12. Black Forest Gateau
Q3. Dundee Cake
Q4. Crème Brulee
Q5. Deep fried Mars Bar

Round 4
Q16. A coin
Q17. A candle
Q18. A barber
Q19. A postage stamp
Q20. ISLE, AISLE

Round 5
Q21. *Pulp Fiction*
Q22. Drake
Q23. *The Great Gatsby*
Q24. The US Office
Q25. *Ten Things I Hate About You*

Round 6
Q26. DANNY DeVito
Q27. BUCKET
Q28. GIRAFFE
Q29. SALT
Q30. TROTTER (James Trotter from James and the Giant Peach)
Q31. SOPHIE Ellis-Bextor (BFG)
Q32. The answers are all characters from stories by Roald Dahl

213

Quiz No. 20

Round 1
Q1. St Patrick's Day
Q2. Daylight Savings
Q3. A monkey
Q4. Gabriella
Q5. The Queen's corgis

Round 2
Q6. Butterflies
Q7. Autographs
Q8. Beermats
Q9. Numismatist
Q10. Corkscrews

Round 3
Q11. The Ashes
Q12. Darts
Q13. Calcutta Cup
Q14. Copa Del Ray
Q15. Ashleigh Barty

Round 4
Q16. *Casablanca*
Q17. *Silence of the Lambs*
Q18. *The Usual Suspects*
Q19. *Sunset Boulevard*
Q20. *The Truman Show*

Round 5
Q21. Snickers
Q22. I Can't Believe It's Not Butter
Q23. Kirk Douglas
Q24. Just Eat
Q25. Hamlet Cigars

Round 6
Q26. Hadrian's WALL
Q27. BOY George
Q28. They all died on the TOILET
Q29. The BACK
Q30. A CHAIN
Q31. BROWN
Q32. PAPER

Quiz No. 21

Round 1
Q1. Tesla
Q2. Reddit
Q3. Kangol
Q4. Wrexham AFC (Ryan Reynolds and Rob McElhenney)
Q5. Swatch

Round 2
Q6. *Shaun of the Dead*
Q7. Sean Bean
Q8. *The Rock*
Q9. Shaun the Sheep
Q10. TIME

Round 3
Q11. Marco Polo
Q12. Charles Lindbergh
Q13. 80 days
Q14. The Mason-Dixon Line
Q15. Luis Suarez. This is the map of his professional football career, from EL Nacional in Quito to Groningen, Ajax (Amsterdam), Liverpool and Barcelona, and ending in Madrid (Atletico)

Round 4
Q16. *China Girl*
Q17. *The Lebanon*
Q18. *A New England*
Q19. *Bermuda Triangle*
Q20. *This is AMERICA*

Round 5
Q21. Fred from Scooby Doo
Q22. Charlie Brown
Q23. Skeletor
Q24. Hair Bear
Q25. Inspector Gadget

Round 6
Q26. Snowball
Q27. Mr Tibbs
Q28. Duchess of Cornwall
Q29. Thomas
Q30. Oliver (North)
Q31. The marriage of Figaro
Q32. Famous fictional animated cats

Quiz No. 22

Round 1
Q1. Gin
Q2. Necessity
Q3. George Eliot
Q4. Suzanne Lenglen
Q5. Al Capone

Round 2
Q6. Simnel
Q7. India
Q8. 10
Q9. Lent
Q10. Where we were baptised and became 'a child of the church'

Round 3
Q11. Snowdrops
Q12. Primulas
Q13. Carnation
Q14. Nasturtiums
Q15. *The Best Exotic MARIGOLD Hotel*

Round 4
Q16. Paula Radcliffe
Q17. Venus and Serena Williams
Q18. Princess Anne
Q19. Kim Clijsters
Q20. Fingernails

Round 5
Q21. Sarah Ferguson
Q22. Rihanna
Q23. Leonardo DiCaprio
Q24. Dwayne 'The Rock' Johnson
Q25. Sylvester Stallone

Round 6
Connections
Q26. M Matilda
Q27. O Olivia
Q28. T Teresa
Q29. H damien Hirst
Q30. E Edward VII
Q31. R Roma
Q32. The first letters of the answers spell MOTHER

Quiz No. 23

Round 1
Q1. Tiger Woods
Q2. Elon Musk
Q3. Manchester
Q4. The number of calories in dishes
Q5. So the children wouldn't eat them and fall ill!

Round 2
Q6. Las Vegas
Q7. *Bull Durham*
Q8. *Funeral in Berlin*
Q9. Grimsby
Q10. *Dallas Buyers Club*

Round 3
Q11. Australia
Q12. Bulgaria
Q13. Cuba
Q14. Japan
Q15. South Africa

Round 4
Q16. Status Quo
Q17. Affidavit
Q18. Caught Red Handed (Caught in the act will do)
Q19. Ad nauseum
Q20. Compus mentis

Round 5
Q21. Bill Clinton
Q22. Glenn Close
Q23. Madonna
Q24. David Beckham
Q25. Aung San Suu Kyi (former leader of Myanmar)

Round 6
Q26. Sanchez
Q27. BIG
Q28. Graves
Q29. Key Largo
Q30. Mrs White
Q31. Elektra
Q32. Bond villains

Quiz No. 24

Round 1
Q1. The Crucible, Sheffield
Q2. Bill Bailey
Q3. Ilkley
Q4. *Mastermind*
Q5. The Turner Prize

Round 2
Q6. On what date did the Titanic sink?
Q7. Name the four albums written and performed by Adele
Q8. What country is comprised of the largest number of islands?
Q9. Apart from the six lead characters, what character appears most in the sitcom *Friends*?
Q10. What country's flag contains the most colours?

Round 3
Q11. Chris de Battenburg
Q12. Elvis Pretzel
Q13. Lionel Rich Tea
Q14. Robert Brownie Junior
Q15. Pepper Middleton

Round 4
Q16. Dion Dublin
Q17. Felicity Kendall
Q18. Denzel Washington
Q19. Lincoln Memorial
Q20. Eric Morecambe

Round 5
Q21. Waterloo
Q22. Trafalgar
Q23. Culloden
Q24. Stalingrad
Q25. Hastings

Round 6
Q26. BP
Q27. Blackburn Rovers
Q28. Nottingham Forest
Q29. Timberland
Q30. Louis Vuitton
Q31. Leeds United
Q32. The companies and teams all have flowers or trees as their emblems.

Quiz No. 25

Round 1
Q1. *Neighbours*
Q2. Quality Street
Q3. Dangermouse
Q4. *Coronation Street*
Q5. New Orleans

Round 2
Q6. Pele
Q7. Twiggy
Q8. Jay-Z
Q9. Kirk Douglas
Q10. Judy Garland

Round 3
Q11. Tony Hart
Q12. Tony Minichello
Q13. Toni Kroos
Q14. Tony Bennett
Q15. Toni Braxton

Round 4
Q16. Avocet
Q17. Phoenix
Q18. Christopher WREN
Q19. Goldcrest
Q20. A kite

Round 5
Q21. 1588 (1583-1593)
Q22. 1034 (1029-1039)
Q23. 1926 (1921-1931)
Q24. 1876 (1871-1881)
Q25. 1854 (1849-1859)

Round 6
Q26. Dancing
Q27. Bohemia
Q28. Speckled Hen
Q29. The Scarlet Pimpernel
Q30. Final
Q31. Huckleberry Hound
Q32. The answers all feature in
famous Sherlock Holmes stories
*The Adventure of the Dancing
Men, Scandal in Bohemia, The
Speckled Band, Study in Scarlet
The Final Problem, The Hound of
the Baskervilles*

Quiz No. 26

Round 1
Q1. Ronnie O'Sullivan
Q2. Scottie Scheffler
Q3. Polo
Q4. Javelin (about 70mph)
Q5. THEY HAVE TWIN BROTHERS.
(Alvin Harrison was in the same
relay team as his brother,
Morgan Hamm won Silver in the
team gymnastics competition in
2004, and Mike Bryan is the
doubles partner of his twin
brother)

Round 2
Q6. *Bridge over troubled waters*
Q7. *Total eclipse of the heart*
Q8. *YMCA*
Q9. *Mull of Kintyre*
Q10. *Billie Jean*

Round 3
Q11. *The Day Today*
Q12. The Spice Girls
Q13. The Police
Q14. NSYNC
Q15. *Revolutionary Road*

Round 4
Q16. George Bernard Shaw
Q17. Graham Norton
Q18. Benjamin Netanyahu
Q19. David Beckham
Q20. Guy de Maupassant

Round 5
Q21. Pringles
Q22. Planters
Q23. Mr Porky
Q24. Kettle Chips
Q25. Pipers crisps

Round 6
Q26. Liverpool
Q27. Jennie Bond
Q28. Tom Baker
Q29. Cannon
Q30. Frank Warren
Q31. Oldboy
Q32. They are all Streets in
names of London Underground
Stations.

Quiz No. 27

Round 1
Q1. Chris Martin
Q2. Maroon 5
Q3. Brandon Flowers
Q4. Marc Bolan
Q5. David Byrne

Round 2
Q6. MISCELLANEOUS
Q7. QUANDARY
Q8. DIPLODOCUS
Q9. ANAPHYLACTIC
Q10. PANETTONE

Round 3
Q11. *Toy Story*
Q12. *There Will Be Blood*
Q13. *Blade Runner*
Q14. *Rent*
Q15. *The Wolf of Wall Street*

Round 4
Q16. Belgium
Q17. Belize
Q18. Bosnia & Herzegovina
Q19. Botswana
Q20. Bahamas

Round 5
Q21. Tito and Hoenecker
Q22. Avril Levigne and Billie Eilish
Q23. Colin Firth and Ewan McGregor
Q24. Bruno Mars and Rami Malik
Q25. Olga Korbut and Nadia Comaneci

Round 6
Q26. Paddy ASHDOWN
Q27. BLACK
Q28. DEAN
Q29. NEW
Q30. ENCHANTED
Q31. RAIN
Q32. Forests

Quiz No. 28

Round 1
Q1. Sam Ryder
Q2. Ireland, with 7
Q3. ABBA
Q4. Switzerland
Q5. Brotherhood of Man

Round 2
Q6. Armoured Personnel Carrier
Q7. Air-to-Air missile
Q8. Conspicuous Gallantry Cross
Q9. Strategic Arms Reduction Treaty
Q10. Vertical Take-off and Landing

Round 3
Q11. Whispering Gallery
Q12. Durham Cathedral
Q13. Rejkavik
Q14. Chapter House
Q15. B. A is Norwich, C is Salisbury

Round 4
Q16. FEMUR is a leg bone. All the others are in the arm
Q17. BOSTON is the odd one out. The others are London Underground stations that end in PARK (There is a Boston Manor)
Q18. ELEMENT is a car made by Honda. The other three are all Fords
Q19. KIDNAPPED was written by Robert Louis Stevenson. Ian Fleming wrote the others
Q20. BISCUIT comes from French. The other three are all from Hindi

Round 5
Q21. *The Chase*
Q22. *Call My Bluff*
Q23. *Tenable*
Q24. *Blankety Blank*
Q25. *Wheel of Fortune*

Round 6
Q26. *Girl with the Pearl Earring*
Q27. *Cyrano de Bergerac*
Q28. *Rhythm is a Dancer*
Q29. *Every Breath You Take*
Q30. TASHKENT
Q31. *Good Will Hunting*
Q32. The answers all begin and end with the same letter

Quiz No. 29

Round 1
Q1. Rome
Q2. New Orleans
Q3. Tel Aviv
Q4. Dubrovnik
Q5. Bradford

Round 2
Q6. Liebfraumilch
Q7. Guinness (I'll accept stout)
Q8. Irn Bru
Q9. Lambrusco
Q10. Carlsberg Special Brew

Round 3
Q11. Roy Liechtenstein & Michelangelo
Q12. Hokusai & Manet
Q13. Vermeer & Munch
Q14. Monet & Klimt
Q15. Andy Warhol & Magritte

Round 4
Q16. A match
Q17. The one holding the teaspoon
Q18. Lunch or dinner
Q19. The lead was not tied to anything
Q20. Give the fifth child the apple in the basket

Round 5
Q21. Harare (formerly called Salisbury)
Q22. Czechoslovakia
Q23. Nigeria (Lagos and Abuja)
Q24. Yugoslavia
Q25. Tanzania (Tanganaiyka and Zanzibar)

Round 6
Q26. Black DRESS
Q27. HAIR
Q28. VICTORIA
Q29. STITCH
Q30. WINDS
Q31. Paris-Dakar RALLY
Q32. The answers can all be preceded or followed by the word CROSS

Quiz No. 30

Round 1
Q1. *The Deer Hunter*
Q2. *Dirty Dancing*
Q3. *From Here to Eternity*
Q4. *No Country For Old Men*
Q5. *The Last Airbender*

Round 2
Q6. GIANTS (Yankees—baseball, Knicks—basketball and Rangers—ice hockey)
Q7. Manchester United (the Glazers)
Q8. Green Bay Packers
Q9. OJ Simpson
Q10. Jennifer Lopez

Round 3
Q11. Cliff Richard and The Shadows
Q12. Diana Ross and The Supremes
Q13. Morten Harket and AHA
Q14. Bono and U2
Q15. Debbie Harry and Blondie

Round 4
Q16. Palermo
Q17. Turin
Q18. Donatello
Q19. Balsamic Vinegar
Q20. Siena

Round 5
Q21. Statue of Liberty
Q22. Houses of Parliament
Q23. Great Wall of China
Q24. Eiffel Tower
Q25. Golden Gate Bridge, San Francisco

Round 6
Q26. Trafalgar Square
Q27. Swan (or Swann, but who cares?)
Q28. The Ravens at the Tower of London
Q29. A gold Blue Peter badge
Q30. Hyde Park Corner
Q31. Cullinan
Q32. All the answers are owned by the Queen (Trafalgar Square, all the swans in the UK, the Ravens at the Tower, a Blue Peter badge, Hyde Park and its Corner and the Cullinan diamonds)

Quiz No. 31

Round 1
Q1. His cat
Q2. Jaffa cake
Q3. HM Sauce or Salad Queen PLANT
Q4. The logo is a silver crown with the festival initials over it (WTF)
Q5. Sussex

Round 2
Q6. Annus horribilis
Q7. Rod Stewart
Q8. King George VI
Q9. London
Q10. Hillsborough Castle

Round 3
Q11. *True Blue* - Madonna
Q12. *London Calling* – The Clash
Q14. *Born in the USA* – Bruce Springsteen
Q15. *Aladdin Sane* – David Bowie
Q16. *Vienna* - Ultravox

Round 4
Q16. Al
Q17. Bobby McGee
Q18. CLINT EASTWOOD
Q19. Charlie Brown
Q20. Frankie, by Sister Sledge

Round 5
Q21. Dante's descent into Hell or Dante's Inferno
Q22. Narnia
Q23. Neverland
Q24. *The Incredible Journey*
Q25. *On the Road* (Jack Kerouac)

Round 6
Q26. Turner
Q27. Mr BIG
Q28. Philadelphia
Q29. Leonardo DA VINCI
Q30. Captain Mark PHILLIPS
Q31. News of the World
Q32. The answers are all Tom Hanks films

Quiz No. 32

Round 1
Q1. Chris Rea
Q2. Mungo Jerry (*In the Summertime*)
Q3. Eagles
Q4. *Cruel Summer*
Q5. *Summertime Sadness*

Round 2
Q6. Maundy Thursday
Q7. St Swithun's Day
Q8. Day of Atonement
Q9. Ash Wednesday
Q10. Diwali

Round 3
Q11. The Open
Q12. US Masters
Q13. Sandwich (Royal St Georges)
Q14. St Andrews
Q15. Catherine Parr

Round 4
Q16. *Driving Miss Daisy*
Q17. *The Hurt Locker*
Q18. *The Untouchables*
Q19. *Out of Africa*
Q20. *No Country For Old Men*

Round 5
Q21. Jeremy Clarkson and Richard Hammond
Q22. Hillary Clinton and Donald Trump
Q23. Woody Allen and Steven Spielberg
Q24. Bill Nighy and Bill Nye
Q25. Carrie Fisher and Daisy Ridley

Round 6
Q26. Dylan Thomas
Q27. Whatcha Talkin 'Bout Willis?
Q28. Dole
Q29. Jacob Marley
Q30. They are places that have given their name to breeds of cat
Q31. *The Man from Uncle*
Q32. BOB

Quiz No. 33

Round 1
Q1. Sherwood
Q2. Jabba the Hutt
Q3. Australia
Q4. Lightyear
Q5. Tea

Round 2
Q6. Margaret Thatcher
Q7. Henri Matisse
Q8. Alec Guinness
Q9. Monica Lewinsky
Q10. Robert Lewandowski

Round 3
Q11. Robert Plant
Q12. Robert Mitchum
Q13. Robert Louis Stevenson
Q14. Robert Oppenheimer
Q15. Robert Rodriguez

Round 4
Q16. Dolly Parton
Q17. Neil Diamond
Q18. Andy Williams
Q19. *Nothing Compares to You*
Q20. *I Put a Spell on You*

Round 5
Q21. Termites
Q22. A baby armadillo
Q23. Okapi
Q24. Rainbow Trout
Q25. Brimstone

Round 6
Q26. Marie Antoinette
Q27. Khrushchev
Q28. Kennedy
Q29. Moet and Chandon
Q30. Caviar
Q31. Cabinet
Q32. The answers are all words
that appear in Queen's song
Killer Queen

Quiz No. 34

Round 1
Q1. Panama
Q2. Belgium
Q3. Germany
Q4. Austria
Q5. Finland

Round 2
Q6. Princess Diana
Q7. Freddie Mercury
Q8. William II (Rufus)
Q9. Ray Clemence
Q10. Norman Foster

Round 3
Q11. Cristiano Ronaldo
Q12. Kate Moss
Q13. Kelly Holmes
Q14. Mo Salah
Q15. Melania Trump

Round 4
Q16. *Blue Suede Shoes*
Q17. Imelda Marcos
Q18. Their logos all feature horses
Q19. Tie knots
Q20. Stella McCartney

Round 5
Q21. *Wall Street / Fatal Attraction*
Q22. *Schindler's List / Casablanca*
Q23. *Titanic / Kill Bill*
Q24. *Forrest Gump / Basic Instinct*
Q25. *Shawshank Redemption / The Shining*

Round 6
Q26. Police
Q27. Clannad
Q28. Marillion
Q29. Black Eyed Peas
Q30. Destiny's Child
Q31. U2
Q32. The lead singers of all the bands above have one-word names

Quiz No. 35

Round 1
Q1. Feet
Q2. Eyes
Q3. Appendix
Q4. Ear
Q5. I've got no teeth in my mouth

Round 2
Q6. *Jaws*
Q7. *The Jazz Singer*
Q8. *You Can't Hurry Love*
Q9. Popeye
Q10. Sylvester

Round 3
Q11. *Mona Lisa*
Q12. *Starry Starry Night*
Q13. *American Gothic*
Q14. *The Last Supper*
Q15. Reichenbach Falls

Round 4
Q16. Archery
Q17. Curling
Q18. Tiddlywinks
Q19. Rock climbing or mountaineering
Q20. Tossing the caber

Round 5
Q21. *Don't cry for me, Argentina*
Q22. *Macarena*
Q23. *Sweet Caroline*
Q24. *Everybody Hurts*
Q25. *Saving Private Ryan*

Round 6
Q26. Vince Cable
Q27. Bus conductors
Q28. Earth
Q29. Flip Flop
Q30. They are all Junctions
Q31. AC/DC
Q32. The answers are all terms used in electronics

Quiz No. 36

Round 1
Q1. Horseshoe
Q2. Ladder
Q3. The crown or the monarchy
Q4. Salt
Q5. 13

Round 2
Q6. The early bird catches the worm
Q7. A snake
Q8. To pull someone's leg
Q9. Once in a blue moon
Q10. A bad workman blames his tools

Round 3
Q11. Amy Winehouse
Q12. Zlatan Ibrahimovic
Q13. Steve Jobs
Q14. Sia
Q15. Che Guevara

Round 4
Q16. Marie Curie
Q17. Alexander Graham Bell
Q18. CERN
Q19. Archimedes
Q20. Tim Berners Lee

Round 5
Q21. Pencil
Q22. USB connector
Q23. Spaghetti
Q24. Gas hob ring
Q25. Paper towel

Round 6
Q26. Their first names are MARK (St Mark's Square)
Q27. CASANOVA
Q28. COPENHAGEN (Venice of the North)
Q29. Stephen MERCHANT
Q30. GRAND Union CANAL
Q31. Antonio VIVALDI
Q32. Venice

Quiz No. 37

Round 1
Q1. Canadian
Q2. 4 x 100m relay
Q3. He caught the bus for 11 miles
Q4. Graham Poll
Q5. Ice skating

Round 2
Q6. Amelia Earhart
Q7. Give up her seat on a bus to a white person
Q8. Mathematics
Q9. Katharine Hepburn
Q10. The Hollywood sign

Round 3
Q11. Ed Sheeran
Q12. Mel Gibson
Q13. Drake
Q14. Will Smith
Q15. Nicki Minaj

Round 4
Q16. 399 (57 x 7)
Q17. 251 (Blink-182 + Sham 69)
Q18. -8 (8 under par)
Q19. 176 (170 + 6)
Q20. 8+8 = 4 on a clock. 8pm + 8 = 4am

Round 5
Q21. The Rovers Return
Q22. Jurassic Park
Q23. The US Capitol (it's called the Columbus Door)
Q24. *Friends*
Q25. You were only supposed to blow the bloody doors off!

Round 6
Q26. Mick Jagger
Q27. Billy the Kid
Q28. Robert de Niro
Q29. Queen Victoria
Q30. Rasputin
Q31. Joan of Arc
Q32. The answers all appear in the titles of famous songs

Quiz No. 38

Round 1
Q1. Sherlock Holmes's
Q2. Hercule Poirot
Q3. Jonathan Creek
Q4. Detective Steve McGarrett
Q5. *Death in Paradise*

Round 2
Q6. Roger Federer
Q7. The Great Train Robbery
Q8. Richard Nixon
Q9. The Leaning Tower of Pisa
Q10. Croatia

Round 3
Q11. Sergey Bubka
Q12. Wladimir Klitschko
Q13. Nikita Khrushchev
Q14. Andriy Shevchenko
Q15. Milla Jovovic

Round 4
Q16. 64
Q17. Mahjong
Q18. K
Q19. Vine Street
Q20. The Gun Room

Round 5
Q21. Fever Tree
Q22. Heinz
Q23. Five Guys
Q24. Cathedral City
Q25. Doritos

Round 6
Q26. Olivia Colman
Q27. Surf
Q28. PG
Q29. Southern Comfort
Q30. Pears (the surnames are all PERRY)
Q31. Simple Simon
Q32. The answers all contain the name of a Unilever brand

Quiz No. 39

Round 1
Q1. *Lady in Red* by Chris de Burgh
Q2. *Total Eclipse of the Heart* by Bonnie Tyler
Q3. *Pipes of Peace* by Paul McCartney
Q4. *Vienna* by Ultravox
Q5. *Shaddupa Your Face* by Joe Dolce

Round 2
Q6. Spaghetti Carbonara
Q7. Guacamole
Q8. Chimichurri
Q9. Lemon curd
Q10. Pad Thai

Round 3
Q11. *Mutiny on the BOUNTY, MARS Attacks* and *Guardians of the GALAXY*. Chocolate bars
Q12. Jonathan Pryce, Shirley Bassey and Dylan Thomas are all Welsh
Q13. EDWARD ELGAR (Alan Alda – AA, Bill Bryson – BB, Charlotte Church – CC, Doris Day – DD)
Q14. GUINNESS (McWhirter brothers, founders of the Guinness Book of Records / 119 seconds to pour the perfect pint of Guinness / *The Man in the White Suit* starred Alec Guinness)
Q15. Davis Essex, Toyah and New Model Army all sang *BRAVE NEW WORLD*

Round 4
Q16. Dog
Q17. Ash
Q18. Vauxhall Corsa
Q19. Manchester United
Q20. One penny

Round 5
Q21. The Jam
Q22. Queen
Q23. Pet Shop Boys
Q24. Erasure
Q25. Yazoo

Round 6
Q26. Richardson
Q27. Pemberton
Q28. Bobby GEORGE
Q29. King (A KING in New York)
Q30. Carney
Q31. Bailey
Q32. The answers make up the last six governors of the Bank of England, including the current governor: Gordon Richardson, Robin Leigh-Pemberton, Eddie George, Mervyn King, Mark Carney, Andrew Bailey

Quiz No. 40

Round 1
Q1. Peter Pan
Q2. Palindrome
Q3. *The Tale of the Pie and the Patty Pan*
Q4. Pink Floyd (that's *Comfortably Numb*)
Q5. ? (sPike milligan and Peter Sellers)

Round 2
Q6. Orange
Q7. Bloomingdale's
Q8. Palaeontologist
Q9. Chandler
Q10. Ursula

Round 3
Q11. Scar
Q12. Chip
Q13. Flounder
Q14. Gus
Q15. John Smith

Round 4
Q16. Zinc
Q17. Tin
Q18. Chromium
Q19. Amalgam
Q20. BIRMABRIGHT

Round 5
Q21. Great Dane and Siamese
Q22. Jay and Rattlesnake
Q23. Lynx and Black Widow Spider
Q24. Moose (or Elk) and Ostrich
Q25. Millipede and Koi carp

Round 6
Q26. Cambridge
Q27. Doncaster
Q28. Amsterdam
Q29. Michael Jordan
Q30. Moscow
Q31. India
Q32. The answers are all cities or countries named after rivers.

Quiz No. 41

Round 1
Q1. A suggestive lump of clay on a potter's wheel in the film *Ghost*
Q2. *Groundhog Day*
Q3. *Good Morning, Vietnam*
Q4. *The King's Speech*
Q5. *The Thomas Crown Affair*

Round 2
Q6. Nick Cave and the Bad Seeds
Q7. The Garrison
Q8. *Who Wants to Be a Millionaire?*
Q9. Ozzy Ozborne
Q10. *Wuthering Heights*

Round 3
Q11. *Into the Groove*
Q12. *Billie Jean*
Q13. *I Bet You Look Good On The Dancefloor*
Q14. *Rhinestone Cowboy*
Q15. *Like A Prayer*

Round 4
Q16. High Jump
Q17. Panenka
Q18. Johann Cruyff
Q19. Simone Biles
Q20. BMX Freestyle

Round 5
Q21. Opposite sides of a dice add up to 7, so three can't be adjacent to four
Q22. Two moons
Q23. Vehicles in the UK travel on the left, not the right
Q24. Vampires have no reflection
Q25. The park bench has no seat

Round 6
Q26. GREAT WALL of China
Q27. MORGAN Freeman
Q28. PLYMOUTH
Q29. Amanda HOLDEN
Q30. PROTON
Q31. GENESIS
Q32. They are all makes of automobile

Quiz No. 42

Round 1
Q1. Apple
Q2. Tomato
Q3. Carrot
Q4. Strawberry
Q5. Rhubarb

Round 2
Q6. 10p
Q7. A2
Q8. The Bayeux Tapestry
Q9. A basketball hoop
Q10. Hadrian's Wall

Round 3
Q11. Fever Tree / English Heritage
Q12. Waitrose / Tommy Hilfiger
Q13. Seven-11 / Dominos
Q14. Cartoon Network / Bic
Q15. Texaco / Total

Round 4
Q16. Three Degrees
Q17. Westlife
Q18. Crowded House
Q19. Kings of Leon
Q20. All Saints

Round 5
Q21. Zinedine Zidane headbutts Marco Materazzi and gets sent off in the 2006 World Cup final
Q22. His pole snapped into three pieces, but he remained unscathed
Q23. Usain Bolt gets Segwayed
Q24. He punched himself in the face
Q25. David Beckham

Round 6
Q26. *Gimme, Gimme, Gimme!*
Q27. Carey Mulligan
Q28. *Iron Age*
Q29. Lie
Q30. Hook
Q31. Green
Q32. The answers are all golfing terms

Quiz No. 43

Round 1
Q1. 1952
Q2. Arsenal
Q3. Horse
Q4. Ration coupons
Q5. 21 April (1926)

Round 2
Q6. James Earl Jones
Q7. Orson Welles
Q8. Vincent Price
Q9. Vultures
Q10. Stephen Fry

Round 3
Q11. Ostrich
Q12. Koala
Q13. Goat
Q14. Lion
Q15. Swan

Round 4
Q16. The Queen Vic (Eastenders)
Q17. Queen Anne
Q18. Queen of New Orleans
Q19. Austrian
Q20. Helen Mirren

Round 5
Q21. Ayrton Senna
Q22. Martina Navratilova
Q23. Castor Semenya
Q24. Beth Tweddle
Q25. Eugenie Bouchard

Round 6
Q26. They are all set
predominantly in hotels
Q27. India
Q28. Mike Oldfield
Q29. Sierra Madre
Q30. Charlie and the Chocolate
Factory
Q31. Lima
Q32. The answers are all from
the NATO phonetic alphabet

Quiz No. 44

Round 1
Q1. *West End Girls* by The Pet Shop Boys
Q2. *Dirty Dancing*
Q3. *Moby Dick*
Q4. *1984*
Q5. *Trainspotting*

Round 2
Q6. Gwyneth Paltrow and Chris Martin
Q7. Madonna and Guy Ritchie
Q8. Den Watts served papers to Angie Watts in Eastenders
Q9. Richard Burton and Elizabeth Taylor
Q10. Camilla, The Queen Consort

Round 3
Q11. Easter Island
Q12. Iwo Jima
Q13. Volgograd
Q14. Einstein
Q15. Rodin's *The Thinker*

Round 4
Q16. Mallet
Q17. Cooper
Q18. Sewing machine
Q19. Oysters
Q20. Thatcher

Round 5
Q21. Eiffel Tower, Paris
Q22. Petronas Towers, Kuala Lumpur
Q23. Golden Gate Bridge, San Francisco
Q24. Arc de Triomphe, Paris
Q25. St Basil's Cathedral, Moscow

Round 6
Q26. William Golding (*Lord of the Flies*)
Q27. Henry James
Q28. Ann Cleeves
Q29. Mary Poppins
Q30. Alfred
Q31. Victoria Falls
Q32. The answers all contain the name of a king or queen of England

Quiz No. 45

Round 1
Q1. Have a drink (first tot of rum)
Q2. 11
Q3. 0
Q4. Hung Up
Q5. They were all cafés on the Titanic

Round 2
Q6. SHALL INHERIT THE EARTH
Q7. I HAVE A DREAM
Q8. IN THE HILLS
Q9. QUIET
Q10. CURIOUS

Round 3
Q11. Pancakes
Q12. *Great British Bake Off*
Q13. Put your hands up
Q14. Tell me why
Q15. The dog's bollocks

Round 4
Q16. Australia, Canberra
Q17. Morocco, Rabat
Q18. Republic of Ireland, Dublin
Q19. Croatia, Zagreb
Q20. Togo, Lomé

Round 5
Q21. Margate
Q22. Brighton
Q23. Broadstairs
Q24. Newquay
Q25. Scarborough

Round 6
Q26. All Vikings
Q27. Sole
Q28. Baileys
Q29. Isle of Wight
Q30. 1940s
Q31. Thames
Q32. Areas in the Shipping Forecast (Viking, Sole, Bailey, Wight, Forties, Thames)

Quiz No. 46

Round 1
Q1. Michelle Pfeiffer
Q2. Depeche Mode
Q3. 50 pence
Q4. Chess
Q5. Noah

Round 2
Q6. Noakes (Blue Peter presenters in order)
Q7. Victoria (stations on the Victoria Line)
Q8. Welby (Archbishops of Canterbury)
Q9. 122 (on each occasion, you multiply the previous difference by 3)
Q10. 71 (the next prime number in the sequence)

Round 3
Q11. Nando's
Q12. Pizza Express
Q13. Five Guys
Q14. TGI Friday's
Q15. Wetherspoons

Round 4
Q16. Rod Stewart
Q17. Jane Seymour
Q18. Patrick
Q19. Fonda
Q20. Jane Austen

Round 5
Q21. Newcastle
Q22. Dublin
Q23. The Reichstag
Q24. La Scala
Q25. Nottingham

Round 6
Q26. Windsor
Q27. Reading Gaol
Q28. Don Henley
Q29. Oxford
Q30. Philip Marlowe
Q31. Kingston
Q32. The answers are all places you can find on the River Thames

Quiz No. 47

Round 1
Q1. SOUTH
Q2. SOUTH
Q3. NORTH
Q4. EAST
Q5. EAST

Round 2
Q6. Discus
Q7. Archery
Q8. Eric the Eel
Q9. They all came second behind Usain Bolt
Q10. Sparta and Athens

Round 3
Q11. *Kill Bill*
Q12. *The Devil Wears Prada*
Q13. *Big Fish*
Q14. *Little Miss Sunshine*
Q15. *127 hours*

Round 4
Q16. Girl with Balloon
Q17. A teddy bear
Q18. Spiderman
Q19. Bristol
Q20. Dismaland

Round 5
Q21. The Berlin Wall
Q22. Pink Floyd's *The Wall*
Q23. The Wailing Wall, Jerusalem
Q24. Unilever owns Wall's ice cream
Q25. Max Wall

Round 6
Q26. *Banks Motel* (*motor + hotel*)
Q27. Pokémon (*pocket + monsters*)
Q28. Bollywood (Bombay and Hollywood)
Q29. Breathalyser (Breath and analyser)
Q30. Botox *(botulism + toxin)*
Q31. *Spamalot* (Spam = Spiced + ham)
Q32. The answers are all portmanteau words (made of two words combined)

Quiz No. 48

Round 1
Q1. Spaghetti Junction
Q2. Truck bodies
Q3. Rare Breed Centre
Q4. The UK's shortest motorway (about 300 m long)
Q5. 62 + 25 = 87

Round 2
Q6. TINA McINTYRE
Q7. DENNIS TANNER
Q8. LEONARD SWINDLEY
Q9. KING EDWARD THE SEVENTH
Q10. PERCY SUGDEN & JACK DUCKWORTH

Round 3
Q11. Silverstone
Q12. Bahrain
Q13. Baku
Q14. Monaco
Q15. Hungary

Round 4
Q16. *One flew over the cuckoo's nest*
Q17. *The Untouchables*
Q18. *Cloud Atlas*
Q19. *The Maltese Falcon*
Q20. *Bonnie and Clyde*

Round 5
Q21. Hogwarts
Q22. The Kremlin
Q23. Windsor Castle
Q24. The Cinderella Castle
Q25. Neuschwanstein

Round 6
Q26. Vivaldi
Q27. King Edward
Q28. Charlotte
Q29. Cara Delevingne
Q30. Jersey Boys
Q31. Piper Alpha
Q32. Varieties of potato

Quiz No. 49

Round 1
Q1. Maleficent
Q2. Eastwick
Q3. Bewitched
Q4. Professor McGonagall
Q5. Hermione Granger

Round 2
Q6. 11+13 = 24
Q7. 19-16 = 3
Q8. 15x9 = 135
Q9. 404/101 = 4
Q10. 36+4+6 = 46

Round 3
Q11. Custard Cream
Q12. Oreo
Q13. Bourbon
Q14. Nice
Q15. Lotus Biscoff

Round 4
Q16. SIMON
Q17. PHYSICS
Q18. ACCURACY
Q19. GENIUS
Q20. HELICOPTER

Round 5
Q21. JFK
Q22. John Lennon
Q23. Martin Luther King
Q24. Thomas Becket
Q25. Gianni Versace

Round 6
Q26. JON
Q27. GILBERT
Q28. ALAN Turing
Q29. *MUCH Ado About Nothing*
Q30. SCARLETT Johanssen
Q31. TUCK
Q32. Robin Hood's Merry Men

Quiz No. 50

Round 1
Q1. Lance Armstrong
Q2. Lusitania
Q3. Louvre glass pyramid
Q4. Lord's Prayer
Q5. Lukashenko

Round 2
Q6. Belgium
Q7. Hans Christian Anderson
Q8. Westlife
Q9. Rangers (55 to 52)
Q10. Jeremy Paxman

Round 3
Q11. Greene King
Q12. Marston's
Q13. Banks's
Q14. Fuller's
Q15. Camden Town Brewery

Round 4
Q16. 39 + 11
Q17. 9 + 41
Q18. 28 + 22
Q19. 43 + 7
Q20. 36 +14

Round 5
Q21. Indira Gandhi
Q22. Emma Raducanu
Q23. Rory McIlroy
Q24. Gordon Ramsay
Q25. CHERRIE

Round 6
Q26. Ceylon
Q27. Granada
Q28. Munich
Q29. Bloody Sunday
Q30. Joe Calzaghe
Q31. Tim Peake
Q32. 1972 (born or took place)

Printed in Great Britain
by Amazon

32238923R00136